# Creative Flowermaking

Pamela Woods studied design at the Central School of Art, London, and ballet with Nesta Brooking before running her own ballet school. Her interest in flowers led to her writing several books on the subject of flowermaking, *Paper Flower Decorations, Flowers from Feathers, Feathercraft, Flowers from Fabrics* and *Party Decorations and Crackers*. Pamela Woods is a regular supplier of magazine articles on craftwork and appears on television from time to time. In her studio in Dorset she has a flourishing cottage industry making flowers for widespread customers, and flowermaking courses are held there for pupils to have the opportunity to make the flowers from her books.

Creative

Pamela Woods

# Flowermaking

An Introduction to the Art of Flowermaking

photographs by Donald Nicholson   line drawings by Illustra Design Ltd

**Pan Original** Pan Books London and Sydney

First published 1978 by Pan Books Ltd,
Cavaye Place, London SW10 9PG
© Pamela Woods 1978
ISBN 0 330 25522 3
Printed in Great Britain by
Butler & Tanner Ltd, Frome, Somerset

Acknowledgements
I would like to acknowledge the generous help of
Janice Wolff, Janice Ashby, Vanessa Woods, Donald Nicholson,
and the Victoria and Albert Museum, London.

Photographs 1 and 2 are reproduced by kind permission of the
Victoria and Albert Museum, London.

# Contents

## Colour illustrations

# Introduction

Flowermaking is an intriguing pastime which is by no means a modern technique. Flowers have been carved, moulded and painted for hundreds of years. Their unmistakable image has been depicted in tapestry, carpets and many forms of embroidery. It is, however, the three dimensional form with which this book is particularly concerned. Metal is a medium which has been used for floral decoration in ecclesiastical and jewellery work. Some beautiful examples of these can be seen in the Victoria and Albert Museum in London. These date back hundreds of years but we owe a lot of our inspiration of ideas to the ingenious Victorians. At the time of the 'Grand Tour' all sorts of treasures such as shells, feathers and seeds for rare trees were brought home to England. As the collections grew, elaborate boxes – even cabinets – were made to display them. With the wealth of new, exciting material their inventive minds were put to work and many creations emerged. No short cuts were made and exact replicas were reproduced, however complicated. Some of their favourite materials were the various shells which were meticulously sorted and assembled into all kinds of flowers. The number of different types of flower they were able to make seems incredible. In fact, the two beautiful vases shown on the opposite page not only contain an abundance of different shell flowers but were decorated with them as well. One can also marvel at the time involved in collecting and assembling a pair of arrangements like these. Years possibly, as their poor evening light would restrict them to daytime working only. They certainly earned them a worthy place in the Victoria and Albert Museum. Their feather work is also worthy of our admiration. They did, of course, have access to the most exotic feathers from all parts of the world which we cannot obtain now. However, this is the result of the Bird Preservation Act for which we must be very thankful because after a while birds were only being killed for their feathers. What an unnecessary waste of life.

The Victorians paid excessive attention to detail to produce their replicas, whereas today we are generally quite easily satisfied with a simple, stylized version. The flower image is unmistakably a seed on a stem encased in petals. The permutations thereafter can be endless. Throughout this book the suggestions of flower types are to be only used as inspiration for further designs. So do not be hesitant in experimenting.

The basic structure of a flower is a seed with stamens, around which petals are formed to protect it. During the pre-bud forming process the whole flower is forming inside a sepal case which protects, and then opens to allow the flower to emerge. It is interesting to count the relativity between petals and sepals. For example, a flower with five sepals will have five petals, or one with six will have six, twelve or eighteen petals. This is an easy guide to follow in creative flowermaking. Relativity of size is another helpful guide; the petal should be able to encase a centre of any size. Thus a flower will look wrong if it has a vastly protruding centre or a tiny apology for one lost in the base of the petals. The seeds can be made with a variety of materials which should, in general, contrast in texture with the petals. For this reason it has in some cases been suggested that a combination of materials should be used to create a pleasing effect. Beads are an example – as perfect little seed imitations they find their way into several chapters.

The wide variety of materials available, from fabrics, papers, wires, beads and shells to foils, threads, wood and metal, offer enormous scope for the enthusiastic and creative flowermaker.

# Basic techniques

There are numerous materials which are involved in this book, their common factor being that they are suitable for flowermaking. Various differences are therefore discussed at the start of each chapter, but in spite of this there are basic techniques of flowermaking which can be followed whatever the material used. In comparing the different qualities it is important to emphasize the handling methods rather than to incorporate or duplicate the various procedures. For example, a fabric which is normally assembled with a needle and thread should be treated this way in flowermaking and conversely paper should not be sewn but folded or glued. Following this guidance, treat the brief descriptions at the start of each chapter as inspiration to create further designs. A few flowers and leaves of each type can be followed step by step and serve as a springboard for further creations.

Virtually every material apart from the unabsorbent shells and wooden dried plants can be coloured in a dye bath. Hot water fabric dyes are the best to use, being not only the most successful but also because they can be varied by mixing more than one together or diluted for subtle tonal changes. Natural vegetable dyes can also be utilized: onion skins for deep gold; cow parsley for rich yellow; tea for brown; apple peel for pale pink; blackberries for purple; and finally ivyberries for ivory cream. Simply boil the material in quantities of equal parts of fruit to water and after straining use as for a normal dye. As there is no mordant in this recipe, do not attempt to rinse the material as the colour may well wash away, too.

After colouring, the material is, of course, wet and somewhat uninviting. A fan heater, hairdryer or some form of blowdryer is the best to use for fluffy materials like grasses and feathers. Always lie sodden material on absorbent newspaper; this helps to speed the drying. As soon as grasses are part dry they should be placed in a vase to finish off. If an arched stem is required, stand the damp material in a vase and it will retain the shape of the vase when dry.

Feathers will gently lift off the top of the pile as they dry.
Don't worry, there will not be a sudden cloud of feathers
taking off all at once! Try to resist handling fluffy materials
while they are drying as this could flatten the texture, and
they would then need to be redipped. If the results of dyeing
have destroyed the texture, a little steam will revive it, as
the gentle damp heat stands the fibres straight again.
Again, as these will have to be dried, handling will ruin the
effect of steam.

Painted marks, whether made with a brush as lines, or
coloured tips or dots and patterns made with a felt tip pen,
can also be effective. Material dipped into coloured ink or
dye bath is successful, and a similar process with crêpe
paper immersed in water produces interesting results. Some
materials, like crêpe paper and feathers, will also stand up
to being dipped in wax which dries quickly to a thin coat.
When waxing flowers it is important to dip in and out again
very quickly and keep the object rotating until the wax has
dried to prevent blobs forming.

There are various ways of reshaping the different materials
whether they are curved, curled, punched or frilled. The
individual materials will have their own qualities; for
example, an interesting texture can be achieved by
punching holes in metal, paper and foil. Indeed, with these
materials, cutting and scoring are very important as their
rigidity prevents moulding. However, several materials,
from feathers and silk to cartridge and crêpe paper, retain
the process of curling. This is done by drawing the material
between a blunt blade and the thumb. The degree of curl
this produces depends on the pressure applied and the
strength of the material in use. If feathers are curled, the
process must be slightly different, because if they are drawn
through, the blade will curl the whole feather, whereas it is
only the vein which should be curled to support a perfectly
intact feather. Therefore squeeze the vein over between the
blade and thumb to produce the curl. This action can be
repeated numerous times until sufficient curl is produced.
All moulding is generally carried out before flower assembly,
but in the case of curly, petalled flowers additional curling
may well be necessary to unify the general proportions of
the petals. As an alternative method of curling there are
some materials which will retain the shape of a curl rolled
over a knitting needle; these are organdie, tissue paper and
fine silk. Simply roll the material as tightly as possible and
squeeze the roll for a moment before releasing. Finally, on

returning to the beautiful silk and cotton net flowers that started life in the millinery trade, these are shaped over hot irons. These work on the process of flat irons which are heated to the required amount and then pressed into the fabric on a cushion. Today these specialized irons are almost impossible to obtain, so substitutes must be found. The two basic shapes are a ball (use a melon ball cutter), and a point (try a metal knitting needle). A spoon is also suitable but remember to choose non-precious metal ones as they are to be heated. Apart from the rolled edge, the spoon would make a cup shape if pressed into the centre, and a frilly edge would emerge if the knitting needle was pressed in radiating lines all along the edge. With crêpe paper it is possible to create all these shapes by easing the crinkles apart or curling the paper by hand. A frilly edge is also a simple procedure, achieved by easing the crinkles apart all round the edge.

There are several ways of making flowers, the simplest of which is where an object like a cone, teasel or polystyrene ball is used as a receptacle for petals. These are simply secured with glue and the permutations are endless. However, the most common method is to use two gauges of wire, the thicker one for the stem and the thinner, or binding, wire to attach stamens and petals. Before any flower is started it is essential to anchor the binding wire to the top of the stem by twisting it tightly round a few times. If this slips, it may help the beginner to make a small hook on the top of the stem and bind the wire around that. This may be a little bulky and should be avoided as the flowermaking becomes proficient. This binding area is termed the flowermaking mechanic and should at all times be as small, neat, and tidy as possible. To achieve this effect, make the binding as tight as possible. This will prevent the flower from falling to pieces when it is complete. Also keep the number of twists for each additional item to the minimum. In fact, if the centre is a very simple one like, for example, a few fronds of peacock, these can be neatly attached by rotating the stem, peacock and binding wire between the thumb and forefinger. When attaching any other separate parts, it is important to have control over the final shape of the flower. Compare the size and position of the top visible part of the petal. Forget the bottom which is to be cut off anyway. Hold the petal very firmly in place with one hand while binding with the other. On no account allow the petal to rotate with the binding. If it does, it means that the hand holding it is allowing it to move. Also pay attention to the surface of the petal to see that it is on a level plane with the others. If the finished bloom does not live up to expectations it is not beyond restoration, but it is better to complete the stem and binding before starting repair work. Then hold the flower at the binding area to safeguard against pulling the petals out altogether. Adjust each petal from the base, at the binding point, until they are satisfactorily arranged. Not much progress can be made if the tips of feathers are pulled into position because they will inevitably spring back into the original position.

The stem binding is a process which is common to all types of flowers except those dried plants which retain their natural stems. To tidy up the binding mechanics, trim away every bit of spare material. Then, using flowermaking tape, raffia, or crêpe paper cut into a ribbon, cover the bulky area. Rotate the stem several times until the area has sufficient covering. Working down the stem keep it rotating until the binding goes right off the end. An extra twist should be sufficient to break the tape. Like all other stages in the process of flowermaking, tie the binding as tight as possible – with practice you will be able to use just enough tape to cover the stem. The stretch in the crêpe flower tape and crêpe paper is excellent, as it grips the stem during the binding. Once the stem is covered it is ready to be curved into the realistic shape required. If a stem wire is to be attached by glue to a puff ball or leaf shape it should be covered first, as the plain wire comes unstuck and will rotate frustratingly. A similar situation occurs when two stems are joined together, as, for example, in a spray, so make sure that the two covered stems are joined together for stability.

Leaves need different treatment, apart from the stem binding, which is, of course, the same. Large single items can be attached by tape to a wire stem and, if required, assembled into sprays. As accompaniments, bunches of dried plants give a delightful contrast of complexity to many handmade flowers. These can be given wire stems also, for flexibility. Make a hook on the top of a stem wire and place it beside a bunch of dried plants. Keep the short end of the hook level with the base of the plant stems and use the long end of the wire to bind round the whole lot. Straighten the long free end; this now acts as the stem. This method of wiring can be used for single items like bulrushes, ostrich and peacock tail feathers. Cones, however, require a loop which is entwined between the scales.

Now fully equipped with the basic flowermaking techniques, all that remains is to choose some flowers to make. This need not be an expensive hobby, in fact a hunt through the house or garden may well produce some suitable material which may mean instant progress. Then, as this intriguing hobby grows, more people and places will receive handmade floral decorations. In fact, it is interesting to make flowers for a special purpose where colour and design play an important part.

# Chapter one Dried plant material

This chapter is concerned with the use of dried plant material for flowermaking. Being true plant form, this is the only material which can be used for competition work within the schedule definitions of the flower-arrangement societies. Although the flowers and leaves are re-created, the material is basically plant form. There is a wealth of varieties to choose, from grasses, twigs and leaves, to cones and seedheads of all kinds. Whether they are used fresh or dried, there are times when flexibility is essential. This can be achieved by soaking or treating them with glycerine when they are fresh. Many of the natural colours are beautifully gentle, and combined they make subtle mixtures. However, where more bright colours are required, absorbent material can be submerged in a colour. Hot water fabric dyes are the most successful to use but if the material is woody, and therefore inabsorbent, an aerosol paint can be used to obtain the required colour. This is usually seen at Christmas when the cones and other plant materials are often sprayed with metallic paint. Clear varnish emphasizes the natural quality, particularly on wooden surfaces like fircones, as the grain is emphasized. A little glitter powder can be added while the varnish is wet to give a delicate sparkle for candlelight designs. The shapes of plant material are roughly divided into three shapes: round globular seeds and cones; long, spiked grasses; and twigs or flat leaves. Usually the seeds and cones can be centres or receptacles for grass or leaf petals. These can be either bound to the stem below the seed or glued between the layers. Some seed cases, like sycamore wings and honesty, are flat so should be treated as leaves. For tiny flowers even seeds from oats can be used, or sunflowers could be attached as petals to harestail grasses. Some cases, like those of knapweed and beech, remain after the seeds have blown, and so could be used as receptacles.

The thistle family, and in particular the artichoke, can be pulled to pieces, and a wealth of different shapes provide an invitation for exotic creations. With the importation of

## Flowers
Cut poppy seed flower
Daisy
Lotus cup flower
Snowdrop
Artichoke daisy
Hydrangea
Harebell
Hollyhock
Fircone flower
Larch daisy
Beech rose
Grass daisy

## Leaves
Giant wheathead
Reshaped grasses
Decorated teasel

## Display
Dried flowers
Dried display
Dried design
Dried arrangement

dried plants from many parts of the world, a vast variety of material is available. At home, a walk in the countryside will often provide more items for the enthusiastic collector.

Dried plant material is very fragile and should not only be treated with care but also its shape should be respected. Therefore, any flowers, whether they are single or multisprays, arc a wealth of available material. Plant materials are always a challenge, from which endless permutations can emerge, so experiment with them in various quantities, directions and combinations. The flowers illustrated in this chapter are examples of a few combinations taken from a vast range of plant material.

# Cut poppy seed flower

Large dried poppy seed
Glixias
Glue

Cut the floret off the top of the poppy seed and retain it, if possible, in one piece. Cut the open sides of the seed case into points to resemble little stiff petals (figure 1). Stick the floret to the base inside the poppy seed. Using only the heads of the glixias, apply a ring of glue to the area around the floret and attach a circle of little flowers (figure 2). If the poppy stem is intact, and is the shape you require, then there is no need to add any more material. However, it is of course possible to cut the natural stem very short and add a wire to one before binding the two together.

Fig. 1          Fig. 2

# Daisy

| Sisam petals | Tape |
| Seeds | Card |
| Stem wire | Glue |

Cut two little card discs 2·5 cm (1 in) in diameter and make a hole in the centre of each. Apply glue to the entire surface of one and attach the separated twisted seeds (figure 1). Arrange them to radiate evenly and leave them to

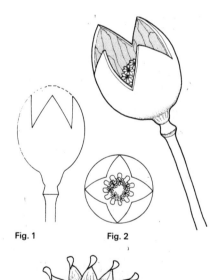

Fig. 1

dry. Repeat the process to create two identical layers. Thread them on to the stem and cover below with tape to retain the position, using a little glue if necessary. If there is a gap between the petals and centre, add a few extra petals by pushing in a little glue between the two and positioning the petals.

# Lotus cup flower

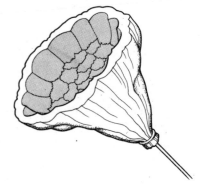

Lotus seed
Paint
Glue

Cut the centre away from the seed and paint the rim.

As an alternative for Christmas, gold paint or glue painted round the edge could be dipped into glitter.

# Snowdrop

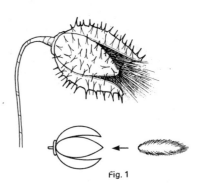

Beech seed     Tape
Harestail grass    Glue
Stem wire

Apply a layer of glue inside the beech seed and push the harestail grass into it (figure 1). Join a wire stem to the tiny stem of the beech seed and bind the two together.

Consider the proportions of the two components when choosing the material, and make sure that they are similar in size. The profile view of this little flower is the most important one.

Fig. 1

# Artichoke daisy

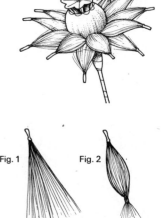

Artichoke seeds
Poppy seed
Stem and binding wires
Tape

Separate the seeds from the plant, retaining the fan with the seeds (figure 1). Bind the open end of one seed (figure 2). Repeat the process with fourteen others and bind each one to the base of the poppy seed. Arrange the petals so that the seed tips to each petal are evenly spaced.

If there is any difficulty in assembling these little fluffy pieces, they can be sprayed with hair lacquer.

Fig. 1       Fig. 2

# Hydrangea

3 didinea seeds
Stem and binding wires
Tape

Remove each seed from the main stem but retain the tiny individual stem. Join a length of binding wire to the dried stem with tape (figure 1). Repeat the process with all the thirty-five others. First assemble bunches of six stems together with tape (figure 2), then assemble six multiples together, arranging them so that the seeds form a tightly packed dome.

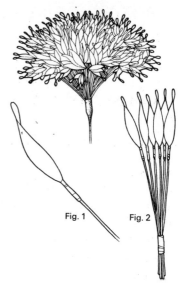

Fig. 1      Fig. 2

# Harebell

Harestail grasses
Butchers broom
Glue

This is one of the simplest flowers to make. Take the leaves from the stem of the butchers broom (figure 1). Apply glue to the base of each and push them between the layers of the grasshead (figure 2). Two rows encircling the grass, of five petals in each, should be sufficient. This depends on the size of both the leaves and grass. If the heavy head makes the stem collapse, then a wire stem can be attached to the side and the two bound together. However, the charming quality of this flower is the weight of the flower arching the stem and facing downwards.

Fig. 1      Fig. 2

# Hollyhock

Harestail grasses    Tape
Dried fungus         Glue
Stem wire

Cut the stem away from the grasses and attach one to the centre of each fungus (figure 1). There is a tiny flat foot at the base of each fungus stem which should be removed. Then attach one fungus to the top of a stem wire by simply binding the two together with tape. Add the other flowers during the binding process. They should be evenly spaced, making a continuous spray of flowers all facing the same way.

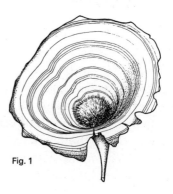

Fig. 1

The only variation which is designed around a particular seedhead is in the grasses or tiny flowers you could choose for the centre.

# Fircone flower

Small fircones     Tape
Scales of large fircones     Glue
Stem wire

First cover the stem wire, then make a hook at the top and weave it between the scales of the small fircone before straightening it out (figure 1). Squeeze glue between the scales for the petals and simply push the large fircone scales into the glue. The fircone is a splendid receptacle for all kinds of flat paper shapes to be pushed between the scales, from paper and wood to acetate and feathers. This is one of the simplest flowers to make. To arrive at a satisfactory design, try to use petal material which is similar in size to the master cone.

Fig. 1

# Larch daisy

Helichrysum     Tape
Larch cones     Glue
Stem wire

Make these flowers in exactly the same way as the fircone flowers. First pull the helichrysum to pieces, then use each petal separately. Apply glue to the tip of each one and insert it between the larch cone scales. Leave the seed on the end of the petals to create interesting little brown tips on each one.

# Beech rose

Beech leaves
Stem and binding wires
Tape

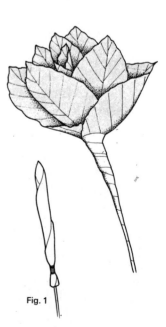

Fold the tip of one large leaf to join the stem. Roll the folded leaf into a tubular shape and bind it to the stem wire (figure 1). Add each subsequent leaf to the stem in the same way. Each should be used in their natural shape and should coil round the stem, overlapping the previous one by half. The exact quantity of petals will depend on the actual

Fig. 1

leaves and size of flower required. Roses can be made as buds with a few petals, or as fully blown flowers with many petals. Cover the wire, base of the petals and stem with tape.

Other leaves can also be assembled into flowers in this way.

# Grass daisy

Grasses
Poppy seed
Binding wire
Tape

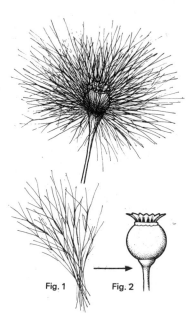

Strip the grass pieces from the main stem. Using pieces which are similar in length (figure 1), bind bunches to the notch just below the poppy seedhead (figure 2). Arrange the grasses evenly so that they form a solid ring of petals. Cover the flowermaking mechanics and natural stem. If it is preferable to have a wire stem, then simply bind the two together with tape.

Fig. 1      Fig. 2

# Giant wheathead

Wheat
Stem wire
Tape
Glue

Cover the stem wire and apply glue to one side. Glue it to the length of the wheat seedhead, taking care not to get glue on the whiskers. Bind the stem to the stem wire with tape. When the glue is thoroughly dry, curve the seedhead gently so that the whiskers make a fan shape, held in place by the wire support.

# Reshaped grasses

Grasses
Binding wire
Water

Many grasses are more adaptable if they are set in curves to produce flowing lines. Simply soak the material until it is flexible. Then remove it from the water and bind the entire length. Bend the grass into the required shape and leave it to dry. This process hardens the material again, and it should then retain the new shape with the wire binding removed.

This method can be applied to cane and willow twigs amongst others, though a firmer material will be required to hold the forced shape during drying. New shapes can be pinned to a board or held in place with dog clips. Experiments using objects as formers, like a pole to produce a corkscrew shape, can be effective.

## Decorated teasel

Teasel                     Tape
Seeds                      Glue
Honesty (cut in half)

Apply glue between the scales of the teasel and decorate at will. The variations can be enormous within the limits of the material available. Try seeds, grasses, leaves or little flowers to build up a close-packed seedcase, rather than an open flower.

## Dried flowers

Wood slice              Harestail grasses
Hollyhocks              Cone
Fircone flowers

A slice of wood supports this mantelshelf design in natural shades of brown. The hollyhocks fill the central area with some fircone flowers clustered to their left. The shaped grasses create whispy, flowing lines with a few bunches of harestail grass to add tonal contrast

# Dried display (below left)

Beech roses
Large twigs

This modern design is influenced by the pot, the curves of
which are echoed in the large twigs. The design is very
simple to make, as the only flowers are the five beech roses,
which are varied in size to allow the curved line to
diminish

# Dried design (above right)

Grass daisies
Long spike
Shaped willows

A simple-shaped ceramic is an invitation for a design of
similar simplicity. The contours here are the three grass
daisies which stand between two long spikes, with willow
bent into triangles to counteract these lines

# Dried arrangement

Larch daisies
Dyed beech leaves

A traditional urn shape displays an informal bunch of
larch daisies interspersed with dried beech leaves which are
dyed green

# Chapter two Feathers

Feathers are as natural as actual plants even if they are indeed animal material. In their very structure they closely resemble plants. So feathers used for leaves can often be confused for the real thing. Not so feather flowers which consequently can be exotic fantasy creations or tiny miniature replicas. The somewhat indefinite outline of a feather can sometimes be used to advantage but, conversely, is easily cut into a variety of shapes. Some feathers like the flat wing, or compact, contour feathers, can be curled into new shapes. The flight feathers of the wing and tail are too stiff and have a better use as leaves or architectural emphasis. The body feathers have charming degrees of natural curve easily incorporated into flowermaking.

Feathers dye very easily and can be painted and drawn on with a felt tip pen. Hot water dyes should be used and the feathers revived, after blowdrying, over a little steam. Tired flowers can also be revived over steam – lilies will uncurl, but they can always be recurled again.

There are endless types of feather available and all are worthy of inclusion. Never feel restricted by the size or price of feathers, as the cheapest ones can be used to produce the most exotic bloom. However, it is essential to remember that good feathers make good flowers, so never skimp time for sorting.

Feathers are available from natural sources as well as craft shops.

**Flowers**
Miniature gardenia
Tiny narcissus
Giant lily
Giant peony
Spiked globe
Spotted tiger lily
Stem of stars
Carnation
Small chrysanthemum

**Leaves**
Hackle leaf
Pheasant leaf spray

**Display**
Miniature Italian jug
Tall black pot

# Miniature gardenia

Mallard cocquilles
Stem and binding wires
Tape

Fig. 1

Cut all the little petals to a round shape and trim away the base until they are a little over 2·5 cm (1 in) (figure 1). Using each petal separately, first make a circlet of three before adding the other ones. When the stem is covered, curve the three centre petals backwards so that they form a central bud, then curve the others slightly to flatten them. This little flower should measure 4 cm (1½ in) across.

# Tiny narcissus

Golden pheasant collar feathers
White goose cocquilles
Stem and binding wires
Tape

Using very small golden pheasant feathers, make a bunch of six and bind it to the top of the stem, allowing the feathers to stand up 2·5 cm (1 in) (figure 1). Cut the white feathers to a round shape and remove the base so that they are a little over 2·5 cm (1 in) (figure 2). Bind each one separately to the centre, arranging them evenly round the stem. Curve each petal gently so that the feather is flattened slightly. When the stem is covered, bend the stem over to make the little flower face forwards.

Fig. 1       Fig. 2

# Giant lily

| Hackles | Stem and binding wires |
| Scraped cosse | Tape |
| Puff ball | Glue |

Cover the stem wire, glue the puff ball on top and leave to dry. Bind the hackles to the stem just below the puff ball (figure 1). To ensure that they all curve outwards, use several together at once because these feathers have such small veins that they tend to twist. Gather all the feathers together above the puff ball and squeeze some glue between them (figure 2). It may be necessary to hold them temporarily with a little wire until the glue dries. Continue the flower assembly by joining the scraped cosse petals, allowing the floppy feathers to curve outwards.

Fig. 1

Fig. 2

# Giant peony

Scraped goose cosse feathers
Turkey cocquille feathers     Stem wire
Polystyrene ball              Tape

Start at the top and pierce the ball with the stem wire in
three places (figure 1). This is to enable the insertion of the
turkey feathers. The goose feathers should all be curled and
then each one pushed into the ball in the spaces available.
The turkey feathers should be inserted in any gaps so that
none of the polystyrene is visible. When the ball is filled,
thread the stem right through the base of the ball and twist
the free ends together. This can then serve as a stem, or be
used to fix the flower to a parent stem of dried plant
material.

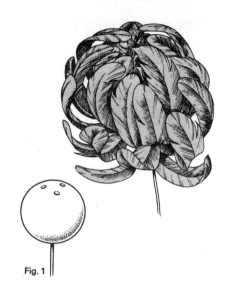

Fig. 1

# Spiked globe

2 shades of chicken hackles
Polystyrene ball
3 46-cm (18-in) stem and binding wires
Tape

Cut two stem wires into twenty-four pieces and use each one
to make a floret. Attach groups of about four feathers and
bind them to the stem. Continue until they encircle the
stem (figure 1). Cover the tiny stem and push it well into
the polystyrene ball. Continue making florets, some of each
shade, until the globe is covered. Thread the spare stem
wire right through the polystyrene and twist the ends
together to form a stem. It may well be necessary to join
additional stems to support the heavy flowerhead.

Fig. 1

# Spotted tiger lily

30 white goose sattins     Stem and binding wires
Green goose sattins        Tape
Peacock fronds

Make dots all over the lower half of the white sattins and
curl each feather (figure 1). Take a bunch of five peacock
fronds and bind them to the stem (figure 2). Then attach
each petal separately until there are six around the centre.
Make five flowers in this way and bend each flowerhead to
face forwards. Bend the stems 10 cm (4 in) down and bind
them all together from this point, adding green sattin leaves
at alternate intervals.

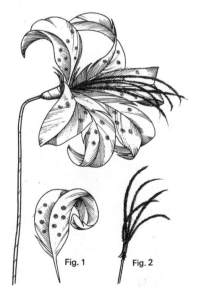

Fig. 1     Fig. 2

## Stem of stars

Pheasant feathers
Duck sattins
Stems and binding wires
Tape

Make a floret of seven feathers bound to a stem (figure 1), and repeat the process with eight more. Starting at the top of a long stem, join each little floret on a stem to the long one, adding two leaves at each joint. This results in a long column of small flowers with leaves.

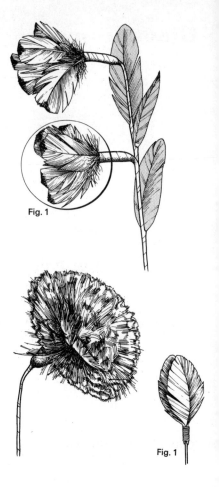

Fig. 1

# Carnation

24 goose cocquilles
Stem and binding wires

Cut every feather base and trim off all the fluff. This is important with so many petals on a stem. Place one pair of petals so that they curve inwards towards each other and bind this pair on to the stem (figure 1). Continue adding all the feathers in pairs, making two circles of six pairs. Cover the stem and then trim the flower with pinking scissors so that it has a flat top. Kink the outside feathers upwards so that the whole flower has a somewhat ragged appearance.

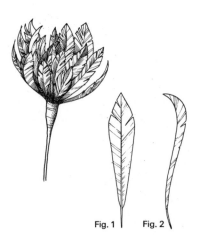

Fig. 1

# Small chrysanthemum

Goose cocquilles
Stem and binding wires
Tape

Trim away the sides of all the feathers allowing the tips to bulge to a point (figure 1). This cuts an enormous part of the feather away, but looks more realistic. Curve each one over at the base and then, by pressing a fingernail into the back of the tip, curl a dome shape (figure 2). Assemble the flower, adding each petal separately and gradually using larger feathers on the outside. Try to keep the top of the flower flat during assembly.

Fig. 1    Fig. 2

# Hackle leaf

1 chicken hackle
Stem wire
Tape

This is a very simple, and really is just a feather taped to a wire stem. Trim the feathery edge, remove the fluff and then bind to the stem with tape. This leaf can be made with many feathers, and some, if large enough, have hollow stems into which the wire can be inserted before taping.

# Pheasant leaf spray

Pheasant church windows
Stem wires
Tape

Pheasant church windows are used here but almost any feather can be used as an alternative. Assemble a stem by binding one to the top of the wire, then add feathers on alternate sides (figure 1). Three stems are required for a spray, each one being assembled in the same way. Shape the individual stems into undulating curves.

**Fig. 1**

# Miniature Italian jug

Miniature gardenias
Tiny narcissi
Hackle leaves

There are many colours in this little souvenir jug from Italy. White is used for the gardenias, and black and yellow tips are seen in the narcissi. This informal design is completed with hackle leaves and measures only 10 cm (4 in) high

29

# Tall black pot

Giant peonies
Spiked globe

Real beech leaves are preserved in glycerine and dyed a
rich dark holly green. This tone perfectly displays the clear,
eggshell-blue flowers. The heavy outline is relieved by the
only spiked globe in the centre. The display, suitable for a
hall or summer fireplace, is 75 cm (2½ ft) tall

# Chapter three Crêpe paper

Crêpe is a word originally used in France for crêpe-de-Chine, a fine, transparent silk which was entirely creased into fine undulating crinkles. This appearance, whilst still available in fabric, has also been adopted by the papermakers. Various amounts of stretch can be obtained and usually this varies with the cost of the paper. The more expensive papers have more and the cheaper ones less. Also, like a lot of things a better colour range is available in the better papers.

There are various kinds of paper which are available in crêpe form. The traditional paper is made in single or double form. This second type whilst being tougher is also often made using two colours at once. Paper-backed foil is also made in crêpe form. A particularly rich-textured form, it has been used to enhance the foils rather than to be included in this chapter, although it could of course be used for these flowers as well. The most charming delicate form of crêpe is glass crêpe, which is, in fact, crinkled cellophane. Whilst it does not have a definite outline, it emphasizes curves as it highlights the shape. Therefore it deserves inclusion whenever it is possible to obtain it. The crinkles provide the perfect material to mould, as the opening of the creases hold their shape. When moulding any number of petals or leaves, try to shape as many as possible together. This not only unifies the shape but minimizes any sharp irregularities. Crêpes, more than any other material, demand attention to grain direction, as an error would result in collapsing petals and, most probably, disastrous moulding. Interesting textures can be achieved by wetting the crêpe and, where more than one is soaked at once, interesting colour infusions take place.

Single crêpe is widely available at stationers. It may, however, be necessary to write to a specialist paper shop for the other types.

**Flowers**
White daisy
Forsythia
Shirley poppy
Frilly spikes
Fuchsia
Giant double rose
Giant bud
Spotted lily
Wet crêpe for giant poppy

**Leaves**
Giant crêpe leaves
Curlyleaves

**Display**
Urn of giant flowers
Curly flowers

# White daisy

White crêpe paper
Yellow crêpe paper
Stem and binding wires
Tape

Cut four strips of yellow paper 10 cm × 4 cm (4 in × 1½ in) and cut into it until it is comb-shaped (figure 1). Notice the grain direction and cut four of exactly the same shape from the white paper 19 cm × 8 cm (7½ in × 3¼ in). Bind the yellow strip to the stem first, followed by the white one. Cover the stem before shaping the petals. Curl them separately so that the ends gently curve in different directions.

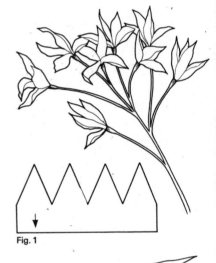

Fig. 1

# Forsythia

Yellow crêpe paper
Stem and binding wires
Tape

This multiflower is a spray with as many flowers as required, each one being very simple. Cut a strip of four pointed petals 6·5 cm × 4 cm (2½ in × 1½ in), noticing the direction of the grain (figure 1). Gather the base of the petals together and squeeze the shape; this makes the assembly easier. Attach the binding wire to the stem, then add the petals so that they encircle the stem once (figure 2). Cover the stem, and make several more flowers, each with covered stems. Then assemble the spray by binding side flowers to one central stem until the required size of spray is achieved.

Fig. 1

Fig. 2

# Shirley poppy

Red crêpe paper
Stamens
Stem and binding wires
Tape

Cut eight petal shapes 4 cm × 4·5 cm (1½ in × 1¾ in), noticing the grain direction (figure 1). Hold them together and ease the centre until a cup shape appears. Use four pairs of stamens and fold them in half. Join these to the stem with binding wire (figure 2). Attach the petals in pairs, so that each one is double. Overlap each petal by half, and place them so that they are evenly spaced around the centre. Cover the stem and frill the edges of the petals slightly.

This flower will be equally successful in many different sizes.

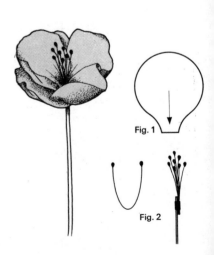

Fig. 1

Fig. 2

# Frilly spikes

3 shades of crêpe paper
Stem and binding wires
Tape

Cut three strips of each colour crêpe paper 2·6 m (8½ ft) ×
10 cm (4 in) with the grain running across the strip. Frill
along both sides of all the pieces. Take one piece, fold it in
half lengthways and gather it up very tightly, holding a
piece of binding wire in the fold. Secure the end of the wire
by twisting it round the stem (figure 1). Arrange the frill so
that it encircles the stem once, then twist the wire round
the stem again to secure it before adding the next one.
Continue in this way with varying colours until a long spike
appears (figure 2). Bind each one below the previous one
but keep the layers closely packed together. Trim the
shape to a pointed spike.

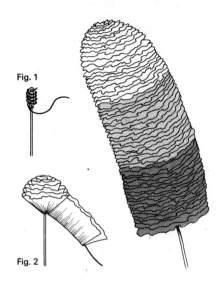

Fig. 1

Fig. 2

# Fuchsia

Single crêpe paper
Double crêpe paper
Stem and binding wires
Tape

Cut three strips of single crêpe 14 cm × 2·5 cm (5½ in × 1 in)
and frill along both of the long sides. Fold one in half,
squeeze it up tightly and place a piece of binding wire in the
fold. Holding the paper in a bunch, twist the ends of the
wire together to form a stalk (figure 1). Make three
altogether, assemble them into a bunch and wire them to
the stem. Cut an oblong piece of single crêpe 48 cm × 8 cm
(19 in × 3 in) noticing the grain direction. Fold it in half
lengthways and frill along the open sides (figure 2). Pinch
the fold until the frill encircles the stem once and bind it.
Cut five pointed petal shapes from the double crêpe
11·5 cm × 6·5 cm (4½ in × 2½ in) (figure 3). Make a cup in
the centre of each by easing out the crinkles and flatten
again to give a somewhat creased texture. Curl the tips
outwards (figure 4). Bind these to the stem so that they are
evenly spaced around the frill. Cover the stem and bend the
flowerhead so that it hangs downwards.

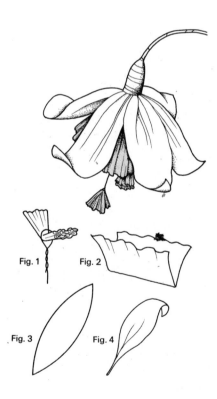

Fig. 1     Fig. 2

Fig. 3     Fig. 4

# Giant double rose

Single crêpe paper
Green single crêpe paper
Glass crêpe paper
Stem and binding wires

Cut twelve petals from each type of crêpe paper
16·5 cm × 11 cm (6 in × 4½ in), noticing the grain direction
(figure 1). Place the petals in pairs using one of each type
of paper, ease the creases in the centre to form a cup, and
curl the top of the petal over (figure 2). Take the first pair
and fold the top over until it is half the height. Roll this up
to a cylinder and bind it to the stem (figure 3). Make a
pleat in the base of each double petal and attach them
individually. Overlap each petal by half until all areas
are assembled.

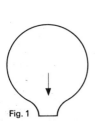

Fig. 1    Fig. 2    Fig. 3

# Giant bud

Single crêpe paper
Stem and binding wires
Tape

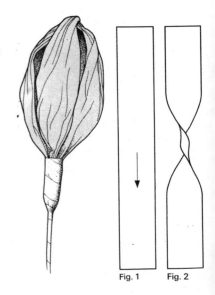

Cut a piece of crêpe from across the width of the roll 13 cm
(5 in) wide (figure 1). Twist it twice in the centre (figure 2)
and twist the two ends together. Twist it twice again, at the
same interval, on the open-ended side. Twist the two twists
together and ease the whole assembly into a bud shape.
Secure with binding wire before covering the stem.

Fig. 1    Fig. 2

# Spotted lily

Single crêpe paper
Double crêpe paper
Stem and binding wires
Tape

Cut three oblong strips from the single crêpe 11·5 cm × 5 cm
(4½ in × 2 in) and frill along both sides (figure 1). Bunch
them up in the centre and fold them in half with a piece of
binding wire enclosed in the fold. Twist the ends of the wire
together to secure it and make a stem (figure 2). Make all
three similarly, assemble a bunch and bind it to a stem.
Cut six pointed petal shapes from the double crêpe and
make dots all over the lower half of the petal (figure 3).
Bunch one together at the base and bind it to the stem,
adding the others in the same way. Arrange them so that
they are evenly spaced before covering the stem and
bending it until the flower faces forwards.

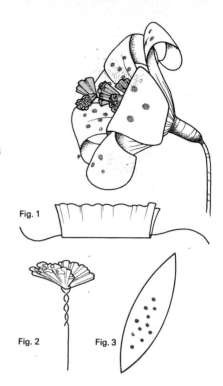

# Wet crêpe for giant poppy

2 shades of single crêpe paper   Tape
Black single crêpe paper         Water
Stem and binding wires

Cut right across the roll of both shades of crêpe, undo them,
and, holding one inside the other, fold the entire strips in
half lengthways. For best results, choose a dark shade with
a light one to allow the dye to transfer. Roll the folded strips
loosely and dip them in water until all but 5 cm (2 in) is
wet. Squeeze the sodden paper and hang it up to dry.
Make the seed by cutting a strip from the roll of black
paper 7·5 cm (3 in) wide and twist it twice in the centre,
stretching out the crêpe below (figure 1). Repeat the process
and work the double twists round each other (figure 2).
Cut a strip of straight stamens and curl them all inwards
(figure 3). Squeeze the base and attach it to the stem so
that it encircles the seed. Cut five petals from the folded
crêpe 15 cm (6 in) wide, frill the top, and ease the creases
to form a cup in the centre (figure 4). Attach these to the
centre, overlapping them so that they encircle the stem once.

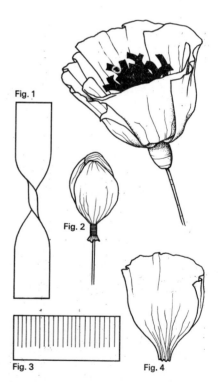

# Giant crêpe leaves

Green crêpe paper
Stem and binding wires

Cut five strips from the width of the roll of crêpe paper 15 cm (6 in) wide. Twist the pieces twice in the centre of each one (figure 1). Join the open ends together and bind with binding wire. Ease the crinkles out to flatten the centre. Repeat the process for the other leaves. Assemble the spray by taping one to the top of the stem, then adding the consecutive ones on alternate sides.

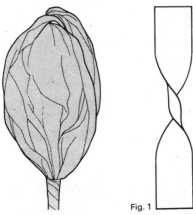

Fig. 1

# Curly leaves

Double crêpe
Stem wire
Tape

Cut five pointed leaf shapes, noticing the grain direction (figure 1). Curl each leaf separately over a blade. Pinch the base of one together and bind it to the stem (figure 2). Then add the others similarly, at regular intervals down the stem, during the binding process.

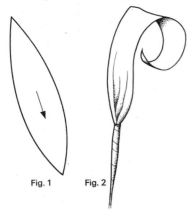

Fig. 1    Fig. 2

# Urn of giant flowers

Giant double roses
Giant buds
Sprays of giant crêpe leaves
Wet crêpe giant poppies

This arrangement is of extremely large scale, suitable for
entrance and public halls or platforms and to fill a summer
fireplace. These giant flowers are quick and easy to make
and effectively produce an instant floral display.

# Curly flowers

Fuchsias
Spotted lilies
Curly leaves

The curly petals and leaves are a feature of this design. It is somewhat Victorian in the way the flowers are arranged in a cluster at the top of the jug. The leaves relieve the outline by spilling out in different directions

# Chapter four Paper sculpture

This is a very crisp and exacting art which can well be incorporated into flowermaking. Cartridge paper is the most suitable, although others, like ingres and sugar paper, can also be used satisfactorily. The various paper sculpture methods of moulding, curling, folding and scoring will create various shapes and surfaces, as will punching and cutting.

The heavier papers are quite substantial and therefore should be confined to the more simple and dramatic designs. These are the modern shapes which should be made into simple modern displays. They should incorporate only a few of these stylized fantasy flowers for an uncluttered effect.

The cartridge and other art papers are available from art supply shops.

**Flowers**
Punched convolvulus
Pendulous bell
Sunflower
Looped dahlia
Jonquil (cone type)
Giant daffodil
Slotted waterlily

**Leaves**
Curved daffodil leaf

**Display**
Jonquils on wood
Brass light

## Punched convolvulus

Cartridge paper      Tape
Single hole puncher  Glue
Binding wire

Cut a disc of paper 30 cm (12 in) in circumference, fold it in half and in half again, and then once more (figure 1). Arriving at a fan shape, use the hole puncher to make a network of holes. This should leave a delicate lacework of paper which only just supports itself, similar to a paper doylie (figure 2). Cover the stem and glue it to the disc from the centre outwards, taking care not to flatten the shape completely as the convolvulous flower should be a frilly cone.

Foil acetate would make a reflective version of the convolvulous.

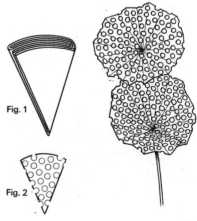

Fig. 1

Fig. 2

# Pendulous bell

Cartridge paper    Tape
Stem wire        Glue

Cut six petal shapes 10 cm (4 in) long (figure 1), and one
comb-shaped piece 5 cm (2 in) long (figure 2). Roll the
sides of the petals so that they are trough-shaped (figure 3).
Cover the stem wire and roll up the central strip like a
cigarette. Push the stem into the roll with some glue.
Gently curl the fronds outwards to make the tassel shape
(figure 4). Apply glue to the outside curls of each petal and
join them together to form the flower. Place the centre stem
through the space between the bases of the petals and
ensure there is enough glue to hold the stem in place. It may
be necessary to find some object in which to rest the
flower in the correct place while the glue is drying.

Alternative centres could no doubt be used, but preferably
in paper, crêpe or tissue, which would only be a variation
rather than a contrast.

# Sunflower

Cartridge paper    Stem wire
Bamboo          Glue

Cut one disc 12·5 cm (5 in) in diameter for the centre and
five crescent-shaped pieces for the petals (figure 1), 10 cm
(4 in) in diameter. Use an object 8 cm ($3\frac{1}{4}$ in) in diameter
as a guide for scoring. Place it so that the scoring lines
coincide with the points of the petal shapes (figure 2).
Gently ease the scoring so that the petals become indented
(figure 3). Cut straight into the centre of the disc and
overlap the join to form an open cone, sandwiching a
looped stem wire between the layers (figure 4). Apply five
lines of glue radiating from the centre of the top of the
dome, and place a petal on each line so that the points join
in the centre. Cut the wire very short, put glue on the end
and press it into the bamboo which acts as a good simple
stem.

The design of this flower lends itself to modern settings.
The weight of paper will govern its size. Any arrangement
using these should not be too cluttered, as the simple design
would be lost if it was overcrowded.

In making pure white flowers try to avoid marking the
paper; any guide lines should be scored rather than drawn.

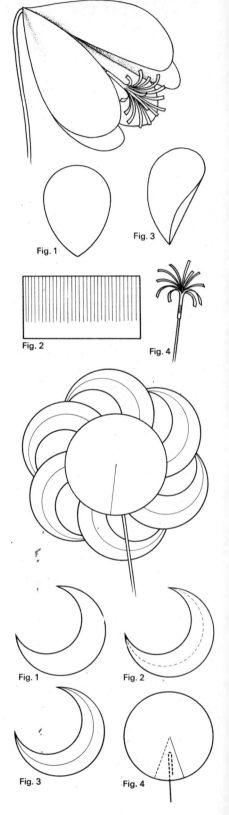

Fig. 1
Fig. 2
Fig. 3
Fig. 4

# Looped dahlia

Cartridge paper    Tape
Stem wire        Glue

Cut out a rectangle 7 cm × 10 cm (2¾ in × 4 in) and strips 21·5 cm × 1 cm (8½ in × ½ in). Join the ends of the strips to form loops (figure 1).Cover the stem with tape, then roll the rectangle to form a cylinder. Sandwich the stem in the join and secure with glue (figure 2). Attach each of the looped strips to the cylinder with glue. Assemble six to form first circle, then continue with the following ones in the spaces.

Fig. 1      Fig. 2

# Jonquil (cone type)

Cartridge paper    Tape
Stem wire        Glue

Cut two discs, one 3 cm (1¼ in) in radius and the other 4 cm (1½ in) in radius, and cut into the centre (figure 1). Coil each into a cone shape, making the first one considerably tighter than the other. Cover the stem wire and enclose it between the fold of the tight one. Thread the open one on afterwards and secure with glue around the stem. Leave the flower to dry hanging upside down. Then, when it is secure in its shape, turn the head until it faces forwards.

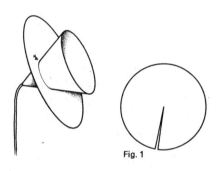

Fig. 1

# Giant daffodil

Cartridge paper    Glue
Stem wires      Paper clips

Cut eight large pointed petal shapes 7·5 cm × 15 cm (3 in × 6 in) (figure 1) and two discs 11·5 cm (4½ in) in diameter with a cut right into the centre. Coil the sides of one disc round to form a cone for the trumpet centre, sandwiching the stem between the overlapping layers. Leave to dry. Curl the sides of each petal to form a trough and join them together side by side with glue, securing with paper clips during the drying process (figure 2). Thread the stem through the centre hole and place the second disc over the back. Cover liberally with glue and press on to the petals overlapping the join to the required amount.

Fig. 1      Fig. 2

# Slotted waterlily

Cartridge paper
Glue

Cut ten large pointed petal shapes 25 cm × 13 cm
(10 in × 5¼ in) wide (figure 1). Then cut ten heart-shaped
pieces as clips (figure 2). Roll the sides of all the petals until
they each form a trough. Place two large ones side by side
to form parallel tunnels, and push a clip on to each end to
join them together (figure 3). Repeat the process until all
the large petals are used, then join the end to the beginning
to complete the circlet. The method of assembly is exactly
the same for the smaller layer of petals which are simply
placed on top of the larger ones. Glue the two layers of
centre clips to make the smaller petals point upwards.

Fig. 1

Fig. 2

Fig. 3

# Curved daffodil leaf

Cartridge paper
Stem and binding wires
Tape

Cut a long thin 'S' shaped piece of paper 28 cm × 2·5 cm
(11 in × 1 in), ensuring that the shape is gently curved
(figure 1). Score a wavy line along the entire length keeping
to the centre and therefore echoing the outline shape.
Crease the scoring so that the cross section is a 'V' shape
and will support the line of the leaf. Attach the base of the
leaf to the stem with the crease folded for extra support.

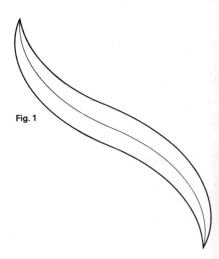

Fig. 1

# Jonquils on wood

Jonquils
Curved daffodil leaves

Various harmonious curves combine to create this design.
The flowers are facing different directions while their stems
are curved so that they can be concealed within the leaves.
Standing on a wooden disc, the design appears to be
growing

# Brass light

Slotted waterlily

This beautifully designed light has perfect classic proportions which should essentially be uncluttered. However, the clarity of colour and design of the slotted waterlily is a sympathetic floral cushion for the light to stand on

# Chapter five  Foils

Sparkling and light catching, this reflective material can be either plastic or tin. It is exciting to use and provides a shimmering addition to floral decoration, where the shiny quality happily contrasts with other components. Alternatively, combinations of various foils in a design on their own make an eye-catching impact. Some heavy gauge foils are substantial enough to hold their own shape without any additional support. The process of coiling gives immense additional strength so that even the lightest gauges will support themselves. However, if a gentle curve is required, then a wire support will be needed to produce and hold the shape.

Tin, as opposed to plastic foils, has a tendency to crumple if it is not handled with extreme care. This can be an asset rather than a hindrance if it is incorporated deliberately into a design. For example, a ball of crumpled tin foil, as a seed, will contrast with plain foil acetate petals.

Being a festive material, it is natural to use it at Christmas time, but combined with flickering candlelight, a shimmering design in foil would enhance a dining table at any time of the year.

**Flowers**
King cup
Foil star
Cowslip
Miniature bell
Triple bell
Frilly foil bell
Frilly carnation
Fantasy point

**Leaves**
Foil leaf
Origami leaf
Lime leaf
Bulrush

**Display**
Box of tin foil flowers
Bells

## King cup

Foil crêpe
Stem and binding wires
Tape

Cut eight rounded petal shapes 3 cm × 2·5 cm (1¼ in × 1 in), with the grain running the length of the petals (figure 1). Shape them by making a cup in the centre and roll the edges outwards (figure 2). Attach the petals individually, coiling them so that they encase the previous ones. When the flower is complete, separate the layers at the binding point.

Fig. 1     Fig. 2

# Foil star

Tin foil
Stem wire
Tape

Tear off a strip of foil 6·5 cm × 10 cm (2½ in × 4 in) and fold over the edges on both sides (figure 1). Pleat the strip into concertina folds and open them out again slightly so that they can be curved around the stem. Pinch the base into the stem and bind it tightly. Allow the strip to fan out all round but pinch the creases if they have become too flattened.

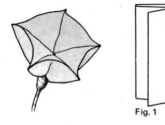

Fig. 1

# Cowslip

Foil crêpe
Stem and binding wires
Tape

Cut a piece of foil crêpe 9 cm × 10 cm (3½ in × 4 in). Gather the long edge and bind it to the stem with the foil side inwards (figure 1). Open out the paper and fold it over to reveal the shiny side of the paper (figure 2). Crease the fold all round and bind the paper in again to the stem at the same point as the first binding. Then, allowing the paper to bulge out all round, bind again to the stem below the previous one (figure 3). Crease the bulge all round and press the smaller shape inside the larger one.

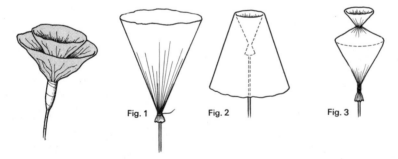

Fig. 1    Fig. 2    Fig. 3

# Miniature bell

Tin foil
Stem wire
Tape

Tear a piece of tin foil 3 cm × 6·5 cm (1¼ in × 2½ in). Fold it in half and coil it round a small fingertip (figure 1). Squeeze the ends together to form a point and bind this to a stem.

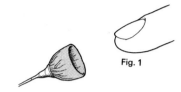

Fig. 1

# Triple bell

3 shades of foil crêpe
2 cup sequins
Stem and binding wires
Tape

Thread a pair of cup sequins on to a wire and attach it to the stem. Cut three pieces of foil crêpe, one of each shade, 6 cm × 18 cm (2¼ in × 7 in), 7 cm × 20 cm (2¾ in × 8 in), and 8 cm × 23 cm (3¼ in × 9 in). Fold each one in half lengthways and frill along the folds (figure 1). Coil the smallest shape round and put the end inside the beginning. Gather the edges together and bind them to the stem (figure 2). Cover the stem and, shaping the second largest piece of folded foil, thread it on to the same stem and bind it so that it hangs just clear of the little one. Add the largest in the same way.

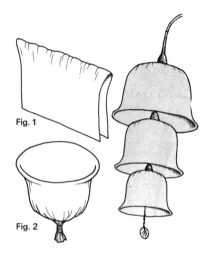

Fig. 1

Fig. 2

# Frilly foil bell

Tin foil    Tape
Puff ball   Knife
Stem wire

Tear off a piece of tin foil 5 cm × 18 cm (2 in × 7 in) and fold it in half. Roll it round the puff ball so that the fold lies halfway up the ball which later has to be removed (figure 1). Squeeze the free end in to form a point. Mark the fold with dents made with a knife all round (figure 2). Bind the point to a stem and remove the puff ball.

Fig. 1    Fig. 2

# Frilly carnation

Foil crêpe
14 cup sequins
Stem and binding wires
Tape

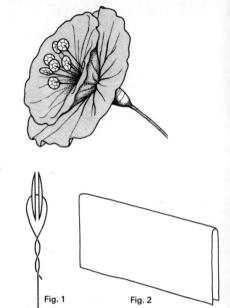

Use the cup sequins in pairs facing each other to trap the hollow centres. Thread one pair with binding wire and twist the ends together to hold the sequins in position (figure 1). Repeat this with the remaining sequins. Cut two oblong lengths from the foil crêpe 15 cm × 35·5 cm (6 in × 14 in) and 18 cm × 43 cm (7 in × 17 in) and fold in half lengthways (figure 2). Using the petal double gather the loose edges together and attach to the stem. Add the second strip similarly, frill the petals and shape the edges by pressing in at intervals with a knife.

Fig. 1          Fig. 2

# Fantasy point

Foil crêpe
Styrofoam or puff ball
Stem and binding wires
Tape

Cover the stem and glue the ball on top. Cut a piece of foil crêpe 23 cm × 15 cm (9 in × 6 in) and roll it round the ball (figure 1). Gather the paper into the stem and bind tightly, leaving equal lengths of paper on either side of the binding. Twist the paper over and up to the top of the ball to form a point (figure 2). Push the lower part of the paper upwards and gather it together to bind it to the stem at the same binding point (figure 3). Crease the fold all round. This double layer should half cover the ball part.

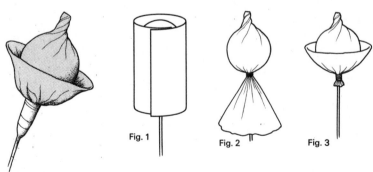

Fig. 1          Fig. 2          Fig. 3

# Foil leaf

Tin foil
Brass wire
Binding wire
Tape

Cut a piece of brass wire 18 cm (7 in) long and make a loop
by twisting the ends together (figure 1). Cover the shape
with tin foil by simply squeezing the foil tightly over the
wire frame. Bind the wire twist to a stem.

Fig. 1

# Origami leaf

Paper-backed foil
Stem and binding wires
Tape

Cut a square piece of paper-backed foil 25·5 cm (10 in)
across and fold it in half lengthways, keeping the foil on the
outside (figure 1). Fold each corner to the centre of the fold
on either side to create a point at each end (figure 2).
Repeat the four folds again to form a narrow point. Fold in
half across with the folds on the outside. Then separate the
points leaving a 1·25 cm ($\frac{1}{2}$ in) fold intact in the centre
(figure 3). This process will reveal the plain side of the paper
and all the folded parts lie inside. Fold the two centre points
so that they meet and all the previous folds are concealed
within the resulting double leaf. Thread a covered stem
wire between the folds and twist the ends together.

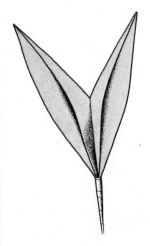

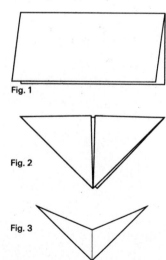

Fig. 1

Fig. 2

Fig. 3

49

# Lime leaf

Paper-backed foil
Stem and binding wires
Tape
Glue

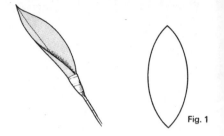

Fig. 1

Using two layers of paper-backed foil, cut pointed leaf shapes, with the shiny sides outwards, 6·5 cm × 2·5 cm (2½ in × 1 in) (figure 1). Glue the layers together, coil the base of the leaf round the stem and bind (figure 2).

Different shades or textures can be interesting for this leaf.

# Bulrush

Tin foil
Pencil
Stem wire
Tape

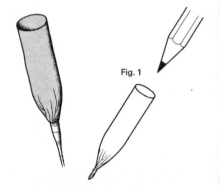

Fig. 1

Tear off a piece of tin foil 7·5 cm (3 in) square. Fold it in half and roll it round a pencil (figure 1). Squeeze the edges to a point at the end of the pencil. Remove it and bind the point to the stem.

# Box of tin foil flowers (below left)

Miniature bells     Foil stars
Bulrushes             Foil leaves
Frilly foil bells

This little brass chest is filled with material which is entirely
made with tin foil. The contrast required for interest is
obtained by the various shapes rather than by different
colours. The whole design is only 10 cm (4 in) high

# Bells

Triple bells
Frilly carnations
Fantasy points
Origami leaves

At Christmas time this display can be hung as a welcome
on a front door or in a hallway. A decoration of this shape
will find a home in the smallest corner. The bells cascade
from the cluster of other flowers and leaves, with the design
integrated by a bow made with folded foil crêpe

# Chapter six  Silks

Translucent organdie, delicate silk and transparent crêpe are excellent materials for flowermaking. Equally successful are cottons, from the lightest lawn to the heaviest calico. As one would normally expect to sew fabric with a needle and thread, it is advisable to stitch as many of the flowers as possible. Whether the sewing is purely assembly, hemming or for decorative purposes, the process is particular to the manufacture of fabric flowers. One of the easiest and most effective flowers to make is assembled by simply gathering a strip of material as tightly as possible into a frill and coiling it around a prepared centre. Gathering of any amount gives additional strength to otherwise floppy material. By a little experiment the right proportion of gathering can be assessed to support the weight of a particular size or strength of material. The edges can be hemmed if the flower is sufficiently large enough for the resulting heavy edges not to dominate the design. It may be preferable to glue the hem or indeed the raw edge to prevent fraying, particularly in smaller flowers. However, fraying can often be an attractive feature and this can be controlled if necessary with a line of glue. Where coloured thread is used for decoration, the vast field of embroidery presents itself. Coloured hemming is simple, yet effective, and this should be the essence of any other embroidery. A lot of intricate stitches may well be lost once the petals are assembled into flowers and placed in a vase on the other side of the room; marks and growth patterns which follow the guidance of real flowers are more likely to produce successful results.

If painted marks rather than stitches are what you require, then there are a range of fabric dye paints which are excellent for the purpose. These, applied with a brush, can be blended and used just as ordinary paints. Marks, patches, tips, dots, lines and petal bases can be emphasized by painting. It is preferable to paint a sympathetic pattern on to a flower rather than to use a patterned fabric which may be too overpowering and confuse the design of the flower.

**Flowers**
Piped poppy
Shaped silk lily
Carnival daisy
Tiny grapes
Miniature rose
Taffeta stitched to puff ball

**Leaves**
Shaped silk leaf
Ball spikes
Frilly bulrush

**Display**
Carnival flowers
White urn of frilly silk flowers

Apart from any shape created by gathering, the petal shapes can be moulded with the use of heated flower irons. The lighter fabrics, like organdie, lawn and fine silk, mould most easily. They hold their shape if they are first sprayed with starch and dried before they are moulded. It is too late to spray an assembled flower of shaped petals, as the wet starch simply leaves the fabric flat. Moulding is done by heating the irons over a burner and pressing the shape into a petal lying on a cushion. To embark on the purchase of specialized flower irons may seem a little unnecessary for only a few flowers, so try some substitutes. Kitchen spoons, knives and melon ball cutters can all be used successfully. Do not use anything valuable as they are to be heated over a burner. These can mould the edges as well as the centre of the petal but it is possible to produce a rolled edge by other methods. Edges can be rolled over a knitting needle, or curled over a scissor blade. The latter can be more variable but care must be taken with this method as it tends to make the edges fray. A certain amount of experiment using all three methods of moulding with various implements will produce interesting results.

# Piped poppy

2 shades of silk   Stem and binding wires
Piping cord      Tape
Puff ball

Cover the stem wire with tape, push it right through the puff ball and twist the end back on itself to secure the position. Cut a square from one of the shades of silk, large enough to encase the puff ball (figure 1). Bind the silk tightly below the ball and trim away superfluous fabric. Cut an oblong piece from the other shade of silk 21·5 cm × 13 cm (8½ in × 5 in) and fold it in half lengthways. Stitch along the fold 1 cm (½ in) from the edge, then, encasing the piping cord, make a second row of stitching (figure 2). Join the raw edges and gather the base in round the base of the puff. You may need to add support with extra stem wires.

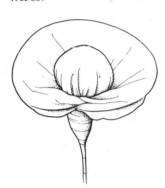

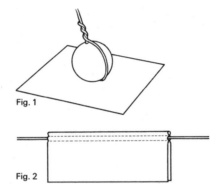

Fig. 1

Fig. 2

# Shaped silk lily

Silk
Stem and binding wires
Tape
Heated flower irons

Cut three pointed petal shapes (figure 1). Heat two shapes of flower irons or substitutes – a round ball and a long spike. Press the ball into the centre of each petal and roll the edge with the spike (figure 2). Coil one of the petals round to form a cone shape and bind it to the top of the stem. Cover the join and a portion of the stem with tape, then add the next one in the same way, followed by the third one. Arrange the petals until they all face the same way, and bend the stem so that it curves away from the flowers.

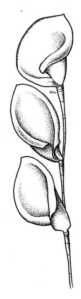

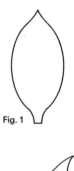

Fig. 1

Fig. 2

# Carnival daisy

2 shades of silk
2 sizes of puff balls, 1 large and 6 small
Stem and binding wires
Tape

Cover the stem with tape, push it through the large puff ball and twist the end round the stem to secure it. Repeat similarly with the small balls using uncovered wire. Cut a square of the pale shade of silk large enough to encase the puff ball. Place it over and bind tightly round the stem (figure 1). For the six little puff balls, cut a piece of the dark silk 20 cm (8 in) square for each one. Place the ball in the centre of the square and bind tightly just below, then gather the fabric in again at the base of the stem and bind it once more. Allow a fullness of fabric between the two binding positions (figure 2). Attach these, as radiating petals, to the stem.

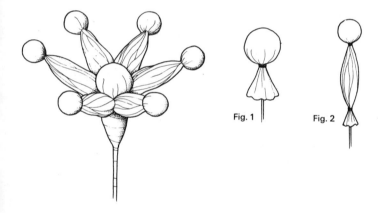

Fig. 1     Fig. 2

# Tiny grapes

Beads of varying sizes
Printed lawn
Stem and binding wires
Tape

Thread one bead on a piece of binding wire and twist the ends round the stem (figure 1). Cut a little disc of lawn big enough to cover the bead and place it over the bead. Use the wire binding to gather the fabric together (figure 2). Trim all the excess away before covering the stem. Make an assortment of sizes by the same process and assemble the bunch with varying lengths so that it resembles a bunch of grapes.

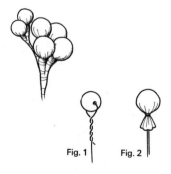

Fig. 1     Fig. 2

# Miniature rose

Beads
Silk
Stem and binding wires
Tape

Thread the bead with a piece of binding wire and twist the
ends round the stem. Cut a silk disc, large enough to cover
the bead and use the binding wire to gather it tightly into
the stem (figure 1). Cut eight little round petals 2·5 cm
(1 in) long and shape them by curling the tips outwards.
Make a pleat in the base of each petal to form a cup shape,
before attaching it (figure 2). Add each one, overlapping
the previous one by half. Space them evenly around the
bud. These flowers have a tendency to fray; if this is
offensive it can be curbed by painting the delicate edges
with glue.

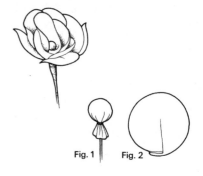

Fig. 1    Fig. 2

# Taffeta stitched to puff ball

| | |
|---|---|
| Watered taffeta | Tape |
| Puff ball | Needle |
| Stem and binding wires | Glue |

Cut eight discs 18 cm (7 in) in circumference. Cover the
stem wire, glue it into the puff ball and leave it to dry.
Thread the needle with wire and anchor the other end by
twisting it tightly round the stem (figure 1). Sew right
through the puff ball and attach one disc with a tiny stitch
before returning to the starting point (figure 2). Repeat the
process until the surface of the ball is covered. Pull each
stitch as tightly as possible to gather the discs.

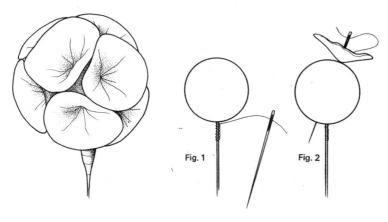

Fig. 1    Fig. 2

# Shaped silk leaf

Silk
Stem wire
Tape
Glue

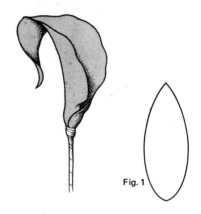

Cut a pointed leaf shape 8·5 cm × 4·5 cm (3¼ in × 1¾ in) (figure 1) from the silk, with the grain running diagonally. Paint the glue all round the edge of the leaf and, before it dries, roll the edges lightly. This forms a little hem which should be pulled tightly to produce a frilly edge. Bind the leaf to the wire stem with tape. It tends to be slightly floppy, but this should be allowed for when using it for an arrangement.

Fig. 1

# Ball spikes

Silk
3 sizes of puff ball
Stem and binding wires
Tape

Cover the stem with tape and push it through the smallest puff ball twisting the end round the stem. Cut a piece of silk 25·5 cm (10 in) square and place the centre of it over the puff ball. Bind tightly round the stem. Repeat the process with the other balls. Trim away superfluous fabric and cover the join with tape.

# Frilly bulrush

Silk
Stem and binding wires
Tape

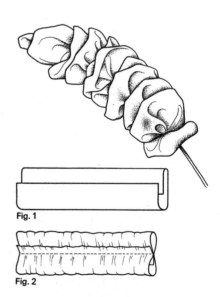

Cut a strip of silk right across the 1-m (39-in) width of the fabric 15 cm (6 in) wide and fold it in three folds lengthways (figure 1). Join the end of the binding wire to the stem and thread the other on to a needle. Gather the length of the doubled raw edges in the centre of the strip (figure 2). Keeping the wire into the stem, and the gathering tight, make the frill into a spiral until a frilly column is produced.

Fig. 1

Fig. 2

# Carnival flowers

Frilly bulrushes     Ball spikes
Carnival daisies     Ostrich feathers
Piped poppies

The feathers have been added to the flowers here to
emphasize the feeling of carnival. Bright emerald and lime
green silks have been chosen for these fantasy flowers where
the rules of flower design have been stretched to their
limits

# White urn of frilly silk flowers

Glued silk lilies
Shaped silk leaves

Silk is a delicate clear fabric to use. This cluster of flowers is
made in a citrus colour scheme of orange, lemon and lime.
The unity of material makes a pleasing assortment of little
flowers in a white vase

# Chapter seven Threads

The variety of materials which come under the heading of threads is wide, from cottons, silk and homespun wool to rug wool, cords, rope and raffia. A thread is generally created by the spinning action of fibres which engage to their neighbours when the centrifugal force is released. Several of the threads will be strong enough to support a certain length of their own length, or loops. Wire can be concealed within the twist on heavy threads to produce additional strength for large flowers. They can be knotted, woven, frayed, looped or simply used in short pieces. Various objects from puff balls to rings provide excellent supports for some designs, cobweb effects and elaborate knotting are the best way to display the material, but often some of the simplest mechanics achieve adequate designs.

Apart from homespun fibres, most of the wools, silks and cords can be found in haberdashery departments. A few flowers are an excellent way of using those few odds and ends in the rag bag.

## Flowers
Rope daisy
Knotted rope fuchsia
Raffia bindweed
Crochet flower
Woolly tipped daisy
Woolly carnation
Raffia chrysanthemum

## Leaves
Knotted leaf
Wired rope leaf
Rope seedhead

## Display
Rope flowers on gold mirror
Woolly flowers
Trailing straw flowers

# Rope daisy

Heavy silk cord
Tassel fringing
Stem and binding wires
Tape

Cut seven pieces of cord 15 cm (6 in) long. Remove three tassels from the fringing and thread each one on to its own piece of binding wire and make the stem by twisting the ends together (figure 1). Join the bunch of tassel stamens to the stem and add the petals made from loops of cord individually. Space them evenly and allow them to tumble at will.

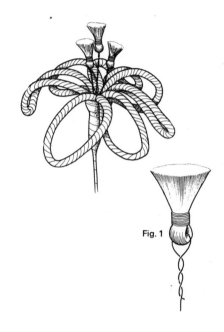

Fig. 1

# Knotted rope fuchsia

Heavy cotton cord
Stem and binding wires
Tape

Take a piece of cord 46 cm (18 in) long, make a loop and tie a granny knot (figure 1). Then use the right-hand end for one extra twist by passing it down through the centre again (figure 2) and the left one similarly up through the centre. Pull tight and comb the loose ends to produce a tassel effect (figure 3). Fix a stem by threading it through the loop and twisting the ends together. For the petals, cut four pieces 21·5 cm (8½ in) long and knot them once in the centre of each. Join the ends together to form looped petals and add them to the stem separately. This is a bulky flower mechanic to cover, so be sure to use plenty of tape.

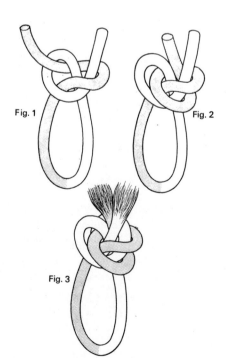

Fig. 1    Fig. 2

Fig. 3

# Raffia bindweed

3 shades of raffia
Stem and binding wires
Tape

Dampen the raffia in preparation for use, then use an iron
to flatten the colour chosen for the petals and cut five
7·5-cm (3-in) lengths for each flower. Use another colour for
the centre and cut five pieces 7·5 cm (3 in) long. Fold them
in half and bind the fold to the top of the stem. Fold and
twist each petal piece in half and bind this part to the stem
(figure 1). Space each pair of petals evenly round the centre.
Notice that all the petals are attached at the fold so that all
the ends are open. For the tendril, cover a stem wire with
the third shade of damp raffia. Wind the covered wire round
a pencil and release, then stretch the corkscrew out a little.
Attach this to the stem approximately 6 cm (2½ in) below
the flowerhead. When a spray of three flowers is assembled
gently curve the stems into a spiral shape.

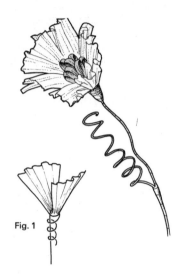

Fig. 1

# Crochet flower

Macramé cord
Stem wire
Tape

Use a crochet hook to work the pattern of this flower.
Assuming a familiarity with the method of crochet work,
start with the customary slip knot. Work a chain of ten
stitches, then make a treble into the first chain loop followed
by three chain stitches. Repeat this petal shape until a
complete disc is made. Join the end of the chain into the
fourth loop of the first chain and finish off. Use the first end
to attach the stem wire by binding the two together.

# Woolly tipped daisy

2 shades of rug wool
Stem and binding wires
Tape

Cut four pieces of one shade of wool 2·5 cm (1 in) long, fold
them in half and, placing the binding wire in the fold, bind
them to a stem (figure 1). Cut six pieces of the second shade
7·5 cm (3 in) long and, making each one into a loop, attach
them as petals to the centre (figure 2). Arrange them evenly
and, using the first shade, tie a knot on to the tip of each
petal. Trim away surplus ends from the knots so that they
appear as tips only.

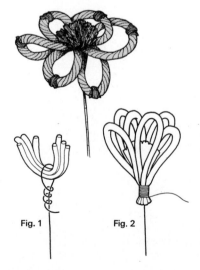

Fig. 1          Fig. 2

# Woolly carnation

Rug wool
Stem and binding wires
Tape

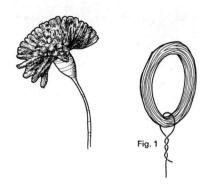

Fig. 1

Wind the wool ten times round one finger and ease the rings
off. Thread the binding wire through the rings and then
bind tightly to the top of a stem wire (figure 1). Bind the
loops of wool above the stem to produce the sepal area.
Cover this with tape, and the stem also. Trim the flowers so
that it is a little flat disc on top of the stem.

# Raffia chrysanthemum

2 shades of raffia
Stem and binding wires
Tape

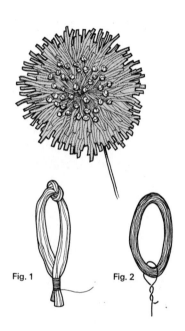

Cut thirty-six lengths of raffia from one shade 17·5 cm (7 in)
long and six lengths of the second shade 195 cm (78 in) long.
Use one of each shade together, and tie a reef knot in the
centre. Join the ends and secure with binding wire (figure 1).
Bind them together in bunches of six and join to a stem
wire. Assemble the six bunches and bind them to a stem.
Bind the third length ten times round one hand and remove
it to cut the loops once. Put a piece of binding wire through
the stem and secure by twisting the ends together (figure 2).
Open out the ends and make five other similar stems.
Attach these as petals to the knotted centre by binding
them to the main stem.

Fig. 1          Fig. 2

# Knotted leaf

Wool
Stem wire
Tape

Wind the wool over one hand five times. Cut through all the
loops at one point. Using all the strands as one, tie a knot
in the centre (figure 1). Join the loose ends together and
bind to the stem with tape.

Fig. 1

# Wired rope leaf

Silk cord
Stem wire
Tape

Cut two lengths of cord and entwine the wire within the twist of the cord so that it is completely hidden inside each one. Place the two lengths side by side and bend them over to form a double loop, one inside the other (figure 1). Twist all four wire ends together and cover with tape. Shape the whole leaf so that it undulates in a double curve. This will be retained by the wire within it.

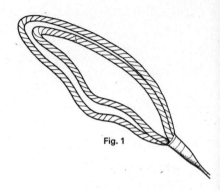

Fig. 1

# Rope seedhead

Puff ball
Silk cord
Stem and binding wires
Tape

One of the traditional knots is used for this seedhead, the bulk of which is the puff ball in the centre. First cover the stem before glueing the ball on the top. To make a flower knot make three loops on the left hand with one continuous piece of cord (figure 1). Bend each loop over and thread it through the opposite parallel lines (figure 2). Ease it free from the support of the hand and evenly pull all loops tight (figure 3). Place the knot over the puff ball, thread the binding wire through the loops and bind to stem, tightening the whole form over the ball. When complete it resembles a poppy seed.

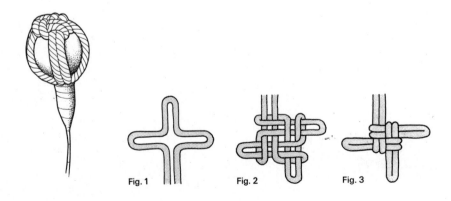

Fig. 1          Fig. 2          Fig. 3

## Large pedestal design

Poppy seed flowers  Larch daisies
Hydrangeas       Lilies

This traditional shape and design is made entirely
with dried plants used in their natural state or
reassembled as single and multiflowers. Natural colour
schemes are always the most gentle to live with and
blend with almost any colour scheme (Chapter 1)

## Hanging pot

Reeves pheasant tail feathers
Stem of stars
Pheasant leaf sprays

The sweeping lines of the curved feathers are placed
to emphasize the spiral effectively when this pot
rotates. Rather to follow than confuse these lines, the
leaves and stems of flowers are curved to shadow them.
All the marvellous patterns of natural colouring are
displayed in this undyed material which is, in turn,
enhanced by the natural stoneware pot (Chapter 2)

## Cornfield

Shirley poppies
Forsythia
White daisies
Oats

This brightly coloured assortment is an informal bunch of orange, white and yellow flowers. They are accompanied by dried oats which relieve the monotony of the crêpe paper used for all the flowers. Reminiscent of cornfield flowers, this display has the feeling of summer (Chapter 3)

## Hall flowers

Giant daffodils
Peacock feathers

These flowers are dramatic and simple, being clear and fresh in colour and outline. Standing sentinel in an umbrella stand they are an impressive welcome in a hallway (Chapter 4)

## Floral display

Ribbon    Lime leaves
King cups  Cowslips

This little spray of flowers would make a
suitable table decoration. By using
an assortment of varying shades of
green the foils are enhanced by
the rich green velvet ribbon
(Chapter 5)

## Miniature picture

Miniature roses
Tiny grapes
Sequin leaves

The gentle golds and
greens of this little picture
are complemented by the rich
green velvet frame within an
antique Italian gold frame. The
little grapes appear to tumble from
the roses and buds which are
interspersed with bronze and gold
sequin leaves (Chapters 6 and 8)

## Hanging ceramic (left)
Crochet flowers
The natural material used for the flowers is hemp and macramé cord, enhanced by fresh greenery and honeysuckle. The whole design is sympathetically displayed in an ash glazed wall ceramic container, made by Bob Parkes Ceramics (Chapter 7)

## Sequin roses in capiz shell box (below left)
Sequin roses  Sequin leaves
Bead daisies  Bead sprays
Sequin roses and blue daisies fill the centre of the box. Leaves and sprays of glass drop beads tumble out over the edges of the box which is edged in the same gold as the leaves (Chapter 8)

## Sun lilies (right)
Sun lilies and leaves
The classical-shaped vase is echoed in the simplicity of the contents. The gentle curves of the lilies are emphasized by those of the vase. With leaves on the stem, the design of five stems is complete with no additional material (Chapter 9)

## Table spray (below right)
Camellias  Arum lilies  Chiffon tulips  Pleated leaves
The wire stems have been twisted together to retain the shape of this spray. The materials used were chosen for their subtle colouring of dusky pink, powdery green and mushroom. The choice of colours available in some fabrics are an inspiration to the creative flowermaker. Being a spray, it could well be displayed alone or as it is here, placed on a ceramic table by Michael Woods (Chapter 10)

## Shell vase

Capiz roses
Scallop leaves
Olive sprays

Every part of this design is made with shells, including the vase which is a pair of clams inverted and glued. A vase of this kind would incidently hold water for fresh flowers. The sweeping lines of the olive wheat spring from the flowers in the centre (Chapter 11)

## Coloured wire display

Coloured wire buds
Coloured wire violets
Coloured wire carnations
Coloured wire leaves

These little flowers combine to fill this china egg c
Coloured wires are chosen to complement the flo
decoration on the container. Somewhat tightly packed, these flowers are informally arranged to intensify the colour (Chapter 12)

## Gold and silver display

Passion flower
Wired foil stars
Ready-made ribbon leaves
Ribbon to tie

This display makes a charming
decoration to place around a
candle for the centre of a dining
table (Chapter 15)

## Tissue paper flowers

Tissue paper roses
Tissue paper asters
Tissue paper fern

These brightly coloured flowers are made to
emphasize the terrific variety and intensity of colour
in the range of tissue paper. Arranged as a column of
blues and greens, the flower stems are entwined by the
large green fern. As the flowers are made to stand in a
pin holder, the whole design is then ready to place on
a favourite tray (Chapter 14)

## Basket ring

Hypericum
Wooden quilled leaves

These large flowers nestle within the cradle provided
by this ring of basketwork from Italy. The natural
shades of the various woods combine happily while
the line of leaves echoes the basket shape (Chapter 13)

## Calico and corn spray

Calico poppies
Dried wheat sprays

This three-dimensional spray which hangs from a
coloured cord will rotate with air movement. The
clusters of poppies nestle between explosive dried
wheat sprays (Chapter 15)

# Rope flowers on gold mirror

Rope daisies
Wired rope leaves
Rope seedheads

An interesting combination is the result of the moulded plaster rope on this mirror which is emphasized by the spray of rope flowers and leaves. The gold rope exactly matches the plaster decoration and is duplicated in the reflection of the mirror

# Woolly flowers

Knotted leaves
Woolly carnations
Woolly tipped daisies

Wool used for this design creates a surprisingly solid effect
but the subtle shades of pink in the carnations and daisies
are interspersed by smoky grey and green knotted leaves

# Trailing straw flowers

Raffia bindweeds

The delicate tracery of these bindweeds create patterns as they wind and twist their way round the glass candlestick. Shades of pink and white are chosen for the flowers

# Chapter eight Beads and sequins

When considering designs made entirely of beads and sequins it is important to take into account their size. Time involved in any average amount of bead threading and the resulting weight of the flowers make smaller arrangements far more successful. A definition of a bead is an object with a hole through which to pass a thread. Sequins also possess this hole and are usually flat although they can be faceted or cup-shaped and in some cases stamped into leaf shapes. Beads are not always round; they can be oblong, square, faceted and dewdrop-shaped to name a few. Various materials are used for beads, from plastic and glass to wood, paper and china.

As threading is the method used for flowermaking with beads, they can be assembled in two ways. Singly, they can happily be displayed on the top of a twisted wire stem and in multiples they form flexible lines. In the second form the ends can be joined to form loops. For a solid form, however, traditional methods of bead threading can be adopted. This involves passing the threads both ways across the lines of beads until the required shape is achieved. The actual shape of the edges is controlled by the number of beads in any one row.

Sequins cannot be used in this way, but variety can be achieved by cutting shapes from them.

Craft shops and needlework shops have endless supplies of beads which provide continuous impetus for experiment with new varieties.

**Flowers**
Bead daisy
Sequin rose
Bead primrose
Pointed sequin flower
Stem of flowers
Threaded bead flower

**Leaves**
Threaded bead leaf
Bead sprays
Bead leaves
Sequin leaves

**Display**
Flowers on a coaster
Primrose corsage
Threaded bead miniature

# Bead daisy

80 glass bugle beads     Stem wire
2 contrast bugle beads   Tape
1 sequin

Thread sixteen glass bugles on to a length of binding wire
and twist the ends together to form a loop (figure 1).
Make four more by the same method. For the centre, thread
first a contrast bugle, then the sequin, followed by the other
bugle and twist these ends together to form a little stem
(figure 2). Join the centre to the top of a stem, then the
petals individually. When the flower is complete, arrange
the petals so that they are evenly spaced. A bud in this
flower is easily created by reshaping the petals and curving
them inwards.

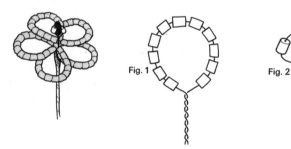

Fig. 1     Fig. 2

# Sequin rose

14 heart-shaped sequins   Stem wire
Puff ball               Tape
Needle, thread

Cover the stem and glue it to the puff ball. Join the end of
the thread to the stem and stitch right through the puff ball.
Sew each petal separately, stitching right through the puff
ball each time. Space them at regular intervals until the
surface of the ball is covered.

# Bead primrose

2 colours of glass beads
Stem and binding wires
Tape

Choose one shade of bead for the centre, thread three on to a piece of binding wire and twist the ends together (figure 1). Repeat this for the other four stamens.

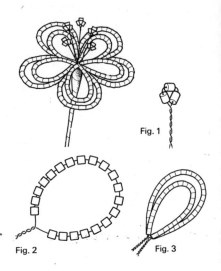

Fig. 1

For the petals, use one colour and thread twenty beads on to a piece of binding wire, twisting the ends together to form a loop (figure 2). Five loops are required altogether. Then use the contrast shade for the five larger rings of twenty-five beads. Join each pair of petals together so that the smaller rings fit into the larger ones. Join the stamens to the stems (figure 3) and add the petals individually.

The resulting flowerhead will be quite heavy so it may be necessary to add extra stems to the original one to support it.

Fig. 2     Fig. 3

# Pointed sequin flower

5 leaf sequins
Bead
Stem and binding wires
Tape

Thread each of the sequins and the bead on separate pieces of binding wire and twist the ends to form the stem (figure 1). Attach the centre to the stem and add each subsequent petal separately. When the stem is covered, arrange the petals until they are evenly spaced around the centre.

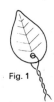

Fig. 1

# Stem of flowers

Flower-shaped beads
Glass beads
Stem and binding wires
Tape

Thread each flower in the same way by passing a piece of binding wire up through the centre of the flower-shaped bead, through the glass bead, then back down through the flower again (figure 1). When all the flowers are ready, bind them to the stem with tape. Place them close together, facing forwards, so that the flowers make a continuous line.

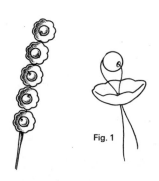

Fig. 1

# Threaded bead flower

Glass beads
Stem and thin binding wires
Tape

Using a long piece of binding wire thread three beads on to it. Then thread the wire back again through two of them (figure 1). Next thread three beads passing both ends through them in opposite directions (figure 2). Continue with four and then five rows of five beads. Finally twist the spare wire ends together. Make five petals. For the centre simply thread three contrasting beads on to a wire and twist the ends together.

Join the centre to the stem before adding each petal separately. When the stem is covered, arrange the petals so that they are evenly spaced.

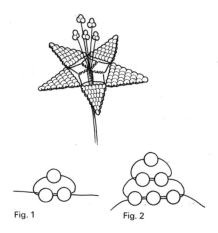

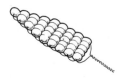

Fig. 1          Fig. 2

# Threaded bead leaf

Glass beads
Stem and thin binding wire
Tape

Thread three beads on to the binding wire and pass the opposite end back through two of them. Then repeat the process with three more, passing both ends of the wire through the line of beads in opposite directions. The remaining five rows all have five beads. Twist the ends of the wire together and add to a stem for covering.

# Bead sprays

Glass beads
Stem and binding wires

Thread each bead separately and twist the wires together to form a stem (figure 1). Make several of these, three or five, and join them together by simply twisting the stems together. If tiny beads are to be used, three or more on each stem would be preferable to single beads.

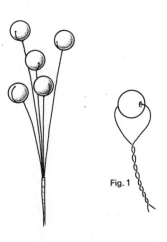

Fig. 1

# Bead leaves

Glass beads
Stem and binding wires
Tape

Thread twenty beads on to a piece of binding wire and join the ends together to form a loop. Then make a second one with twenty-five beads and join the two together so that the small one lies flat inside the larger one. Cover the joined stems. An interesting effect can be achieved with two shades of bead, one for the outside and the other inside.

# Sequin leaves

Leaf-shaped sequins
Stem and binding wire
Tape

Thread each sequin on to a piece of binding wire and twist the ends together to form a stem. Assemble into a spray as required. Some gypsy sequins, the big flat ones, can be used in the same way and cut into the required leaf shape.

# Flowers on a coaster (below left)

Stem of flowers
Pointed sequin flowers
Cut sequin leaves
Bead sprays

This delicate little collection is displayed on a coaster.
Red, white and blue is the colour scheme chosen here, the
cut sequin leaves are most unusual in red. They form a
positive base for the little white flowers and sprays of
flowers, with sprays of red beads interspersed between them

# Primrose corsage (above)

Primroses
Bead leaves

This little spray is assembled for a glittering corsage to
adorn an evening dress

# Threaded bead miniature

Threaded bead leaves
Sprays of beads
Bead daisies
Threaded bead flower

The little spray is entirely made with tiny glass beads. The subtle colouring of green, brown and pale gold is complemented by the gold-thread tie round the stems

# Chapter nine Ribbons

The definition of a ribbon is a flat strip of fabric which is usually woven. In this chapter, parcel ribbon is included, although this is not woven, or fabric, but has a special quality of its own. The outline of ribbon may well seem uninteresting but the uniformity should act as a challenge for transformation.

It can be cut, knotted, curled and sewn as well as looped. The velvet variety in particular is ideal for leaves when glued to a wire support. Often this makes an excellent contrast to accompanying flowers. There are many additional ribbons made of nylon, petersham, lace or patterned ribbon with spots, stripes or tartan, although the plain ones lend themselves to flowermaking more realistically than the patterned ones.

Ribbon is one of the easiest materials to obtain as it can be found in any haberdashery department.

**Flowers**
Ribbon fuchsia
Ribbon daisy
Sun lily
Ribbon rose bud
Velvet ribbon flower
Quilled flower
Peony
Coiled rose
Two-tone rose
Pom-pom dahlia
Velvet lily
Folded star
Coiled bud
Shaded ribbon flower

**Leaves**
Ribbon catkins
Ribbon leaves (fan)
Ribbon leaves (looped)

**Display**
Bamboo container
Glass dome
Basket of daisies
Shaded ribbon mirror display

# Ribbon fuchsia

2 shades of parcel ribbon
3 glass drop beads
Stem and binding wires
Tape

Cut five pieces of ribbon 10 cm (4 in) long and six pieces in the contrasting colour 14 cm (5½ in) long. Then cut the tips of all the pieces to a pointed shape (figure 1). Thread a glass drop bead on to a piece of binding wire and twist the ends together to form a stem (figure 2). Make three identical ones and bind them to the stem, varying the lengths of stem but averaging 5 cm (2 in). Gather the base of one of the short petals and bind it to the stem, adding the other similar ones in the same way. Then attach the large ones similarly, making a second circlet of petals. Cover the stem and bend it over to allow the flower to hang downwards.

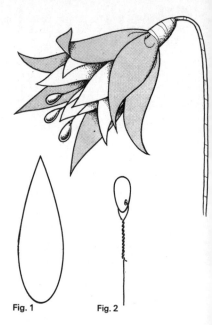

Fig. 1          Fig. 2

# Ribbon daisy

Heavy petersham ribbon
Glixias
Stem and binding wires
Tape

Make a bunch of glixias with varying length stems and bind them to the stem wire (figure 1). Cut ten pieces of ribbon diagonally in 10-cm (4-in) lengths (figure 2). Apply one petal after another in any space available until all are attached. Cover the stem before curving the tips of the petals outwards. The size of this flower can vary enormously according to the ribbon, and the length of petal will be determined by the ability of the ribbon to support its own weight.

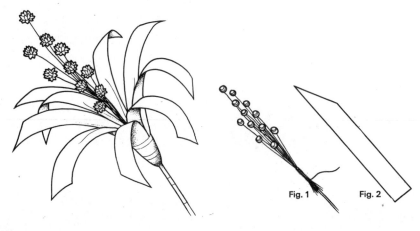

Fig. 1          Fig. 2

# Sun lily

2 shades of parcel ribbon
Green parcel ribbon
Stem and binding wires
Tape

Cut six pieces 5 cm (2 in) long from one shade, and thirteen pieces 8·5 cm (3¼ in) long from the other. Cut all the tips to a pointed shape (figure 1). Cut five green pieces 8·5 cm (3¼ in) long for the leaves and cut both ends of each one to a point.

Using the short pieces first, pinch one at the base to gather it together and bind it to the stem (figure 2). Repeat the process with the remaining short ones arranging them so that they are spaced evenly around the stem. Add the large petal pieces in the same way. During the stem binding process, add a leaf at regular intervals (figure 3). No wire is needed with this and the leaves will coil round the stem. Curl the tips of all the large petals outwards and the small petals inwards.

Fig. 1    Fig. 2

Fig. 3

# Ribbon rose bud

Parcel ribbon
Stem and binding wires
Tape

One strip only is required for this little bud which is created by open folding. Cut the piece 10 cm (4 in) long and fold both ends over (figure 1). Fold one half over the other (figure 2). Take care not to flatten the folds as this will destroy the substance of the bud. Pinch the base of the buds together (figure 3), and bind with wire to the stem. There will be a lot of waste material to remove before covering the stem.

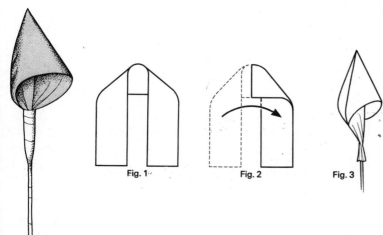

Fig. 1    Fig. 2    Fig. 3

# Velvet ribbon flower

Velvet ribbon
Glixias
Stem and binding wires
Tape

Make a bunch of glixias of varying lengths and bind them
to the stem (figure 1). Cut five pieces of ribbon 14 cm
(5½ in) long. Take one piece, flat side up, and, folding it in
the centre, fold either side over. This forms a cone shape
(figure 2). Squeeze the free ends together and bind to the
stem. Take care not to leave the lengths too long because
the velvet side is the most important, and ideally one should
see as little of the reverse side as possible. This is a very
heavy flowerhead and so may well require a few extra
stem wires joined to the original stem to support it.

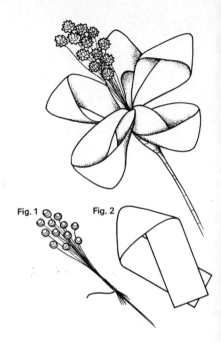

Fig. 1    Fig. 2

# Quilled flowers

Parcel ribbon
1 bead
Stem and binding wires
Tape

Thread the bead with binding wire and twist the ends
together (figure 1). Loop the ribbon with rings which get
increasingly larger (figure 2), and secure the shape with a
wire twist. Make five of these and join them to the stem by
twisting the wire round the stem. Arrange the petals so that
they join and lie on a flat plane.

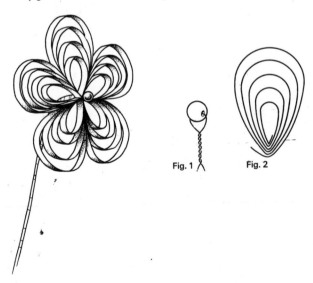

Fig. 1    Fig. 2

# Peony

Parcel ribbon    Tape
Polystyrene ball    Stapler
Stem wire

Cover the stem wire with tape before glueing it to the polystyrene ball. Leave it to dry. Cut a large number of pieces – approximately one hundred – of parcel ribbon 6 cm (2½ in) long with pointed tips (figure 1). Starting at the top, attach the petals one by one by stapling the base of each one to the ball. Add the petals in any spaces available until the sphere is covered. Curve the tips of the petals outwards. This exotic flower would also be attractive in two colours, perhaps one in the centre with a variation round the outside.

Fig. 1

# Coiled rose

Velvet ribbon with satin reverse
Stem and binding wires
Tape

Cut nine pieces of ribbon 18 cm (7 in) long and one 7 cm (2¾ in). Using the smallest piece first, coil the end round the stem to attach it and bind tightly (figure 1). Roll one of the larger pieces over twice to produce a cylinder with a diagonal coil (figure 2). Bring the ends round until they overlap (figure 3), and bind this to the stem, ensuring that the shape coils round the centre, hugging it closely. Continue adding the remaining petals by the same process. The instructions are for a fully blown rose bud.

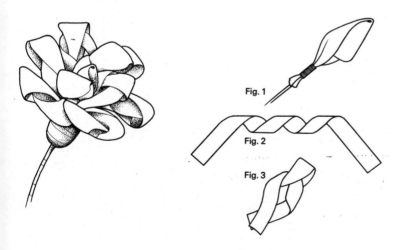

Fig. 1

Fig. 2

Fig. 3

87

# Two-tone rose

Velvet ribbon with satin reverse
Stem and binding wires
Tape

Cut eight rounded petal shapes 5 cm × 3 cm (2 in × 1¼ in)
(figure 1), and one piece 7 cm (2¾ in) long. Attach the short
piece to the top of the stem, coil the loose end round to form
a cone and bind this tightly. Curl the tops of all the petals
over a knife and make a pleat in the base of each one before
adding it to the flower (figure 2). Each petal should coil
round the others, overlapping the previous one by half.

# Pom-pom dahlia

Flocked ribbon
Stem and binding wires
Tape

Cut nine pieces of ribbon 20 cm (8 in) long. Take one and
shape it into a loop with two ends (figure 1). Thread a piece
of binding wire through the loop and twist the ends
together. This not only secures the ribbon but, by twisting
tightly, the loop and ends will gather up. Repeat the process
with the other pieces of ribbon. Then assemble them in
groups of three and bind three groups to the stem.
Ensure that they all have the same length wire stem, as this
will produce an even dome shape.

# Velvet lily

Velvet ribbon
Stem and binding wires
Tape

Cut a piece of velvet ribbon, the florist variety which is stiff
and doesn't fray, to a pointed petal shape (figure 1). Coil the
sides round and bind it to the stem. Curl the top of the petal
outwards ensuring that the base of the petal doesn't get
squashed in the process.

# Folded star

Shaded ribbon
Stem and binding wires
Tape

Cut one length of ribbon 7 cm (2¾ in) and five pieces 9·5 cm (3¾ in). Use the small piece for the centre and coil the ribbon round. Join the ends together and bind it to the top of a stem (figure 1). Fold one of the remaining pieces in half, then invert the edges of the fold on either side to create a point (figure 2). Gather the loose edges together and bind to the stem. Make the remaining petals in the same way and arrange them so that they radiate evenly from the centre.

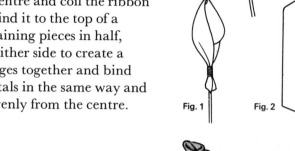

Fig. 1    Fig. 2

# Coiled bud

Shaded ribbon
Stem and binding wires
Tape

Cut a piece of ribbon 7 cm (2¾ in) long and fold it in half lengthways. Bind one end to the stem (figure 1), and coil the remaining length with the loose edges and the binding wire together. A fuller bud can simply be made with longer ribbon, and velvet ribbon is a good substitute for rose buds.

Fig. 1

# Shaded ribbon flower

Shaded ribbon
Stem and binding wires
Tape

Cut five pieces of ribbon 11·5 cm (4½ in) long and one 7 cm (2¾ in). Use the short piece for the centre and attach one end to the stem. Coil the ribbon round and bind it to the stem, forming a cone shape (figure 1). Fold each of the others in half with the right side inwards. Open out the ends and curve them round to join each other but retain the fold as a crease (figure 2). Attach these to the centre, arranging them evenly round the stem.

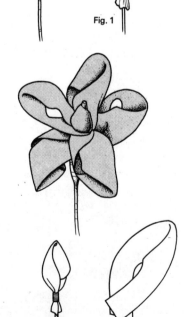

Fig. 1    Fig. 2

# Ribbon catkins

Thin parted ribbon
Stem wire
Tape

Cut nine pieces of ribbon 20 cm (8 in) long and curl each
one to a tight corkscrew by pulling it over the blade of a
knife. Using them in groups of three, they can be attached
with the tape during stem binding (figure 1). Attach the
first group to the top of the stem and the others at regular
intervals. Shape the stem by making curves to allow the
catkins to hang free. The appearance should be of a stem
which winds its way round the vertical catkins.

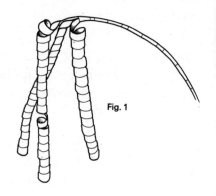

Fig. 1

# Ribbon leaves (fan)

Parcel ribbon
Stem and binding wires
Tape
Stapler

Cut six small pieces 5 cm (2 in) long and staple them
together side by side, so that all the joins are on the same
side (figure 1). Fan out one end while pinching the other
together for binding to the stem. When the stem is covered,
fan the leaf out again and cut the sides down to make a more
circular leaf than it was before (figure 2). This leaf resembles
lady's mantle.

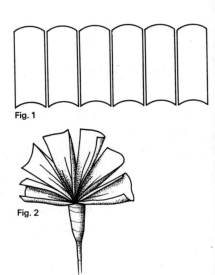

Fig. 1

Fig. 2

# Ribbon leaves (looped)

Heavy petersham ribbon
Stem and binding wires
Tape

Cut five pieces of ribbon 10 cm (8 in) long, make a loop of
each one and secure with wire. Join one to the top of the
stem with tape, then continue binding and joining leaves
at regular intervals during the process.

# Bamboo container (below)

Ribbon rose buds
Ribbon catkins
Ribbon leaves

This unusual little container was an invitation for the
catkins on their twisted stems to entwine their way around
the arch. A line of yellow rose buds is enhanced by the
ribbon fan leaves

# Glass dome (right)

| | |
|---|---|
| Two-tone rose | Pom-pom dahlia |
| Velvet lily | Coiled rose |
| Ribbon rose buds | Ready-made leaves |

These Victorian glass domes are treasures to obtain
whenever possible. They encase and preserve handmade
flowers in perfect condition. The design should really fill
the total area inside to copy the Victorian style of a luxurious
floral display

# Basket of daisies

Ribbon daisies
Velvet ribbon flowers
Ribbon leaves

These informal flowers nestle together in the basket. The colours are chosen to blend together in shades of green and brown and the velvet texture contrasts with the loose weave of the daisies

# Shaded ribbon mirror display

Shaded ribbon flower
Coiled buds
Folded stars
Ready-made leaves

This circular frame has the added charm of these shaded
ribbon flowers nestling into the side. The velvet leaves are
ready-made but, being shaded, they complement the ribbon
used for all the flowers.

# Chapter ten Wired fabrics

There are times, particularly when using flimsy or fine-weight fabrics, when a wire frame is an excellent method of display. In supporting a large area of fabric it is possible to enjoy the finer qualities of translucency and subtle weave. Whether the wire is used to retain a flat-shaped petal or keep the perimeter of a gathered shape, it is possible to use flowers of immense variety of size subject to the strength of the wire. Any moulding of petal or leaf shape is made by bending the wire.

There are two types of material which are suitable for wire frames and this depends on which method is to be used, the flat or gathered shape. Virtually any material, from the heaviest brocades to the finest silks, are suitable for the flat shape, which is stitched and then reversed. Essentially the material should not be transparent, as the unsightly raw edges inside might show through. However, the transparent quality is ideal for fabrics gathered within a frame. The layers are then all clearly visible. If a solid fabric is preferable, try to choose a shiny satin or silk so that the light will emphasize the folds.

Various types of wire can be used from milliners' such as copper, brass and silver jewellery wire. Some of the latter may be an unnecessary extravagance but the choice is really dependent on the fabric to be supported. It should be remembered that wire has various strengths and an ideal one to choose would be a fine, strong one which does not collapse easily. If the fabric is very transparent, then the wire, being clearly visible, plays a prominent part in the design, and colour is important.

There is no need to suggest where fabric is available but the wire may prove to be a little more difficult. Haberdashery departments usually have milliners' wire, as do craft and hobby shops.

**Flowers**
Fantasy bud
Arum lily
Table flower
Chiffon tulip
Tiger lily
Camellia
Patterned cone

**Leaves**
Brocade leaf
Pleated leaf

**Display**
Table flower display
Tea urn

# Fantasy bud

Fine silk
Brass wire
Stem and binding wires
Tape

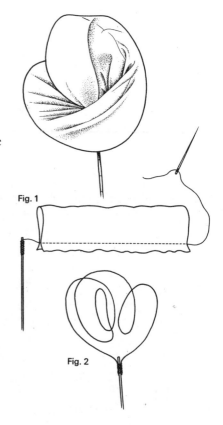

Cut an oblong piece of silk 25·5 cm × 12·5 cm (10 in × 5 in)
and fold it in half lengthways. Twist one end of binding wire
round the end of the stem wire and thread a needle on to
the other. Gather along the long open sides stitching
through both layers at once (figure 1). Pull up as tightly as
possible and thread the end of the brass wire through the
loose fold, leaving extra wire on both sides of the fabric.
Then gently ease the wire into the fabric until it forms loops
and twists around itself (figure 2). Secure the ends when a
satisfactory shape has been created. This interesting fantasy
shape often turns out differently every time it is made.

# Arum lily

5 glass drop beads    Stem and binding wires
Silk    Tape
Brass wire

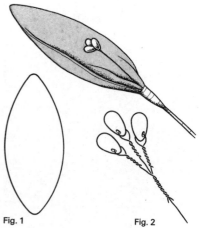

Cut two pointed oval shapes from the silk, remembering to
cut one shape from either side of the fabric (figure 1). Face
the wrong sides together and stitch all round the edges
before turning it inside out to reveal the right side. Make a
slightly pointed loop with the brass wire and push it into the
petal shape until the fabric is stretched. Secure the shape
and fabric by binding very tightly. The seed-centre is made
with three glass drop beads which are threaded on to their
own individual binding wire stem (figure 2). Bunch them
together and bind them to the petal binding. Cover the stem
and coil the petal shape round the seeds slightly.

# Table flower

¼ m silk chiffon        Stem and binding wires
30 glass drop beads     Tape
Brass wire

Cut the chiffon into fifteen squares 28 cm (11 in) across,
and cut a piece of brass wire for each one 30 cm (12 in) long.
Prepare each petal by threading a needle with binding wire
and twist the end round the piece of brass wire to secure it.
Fold a piece of fabric in half diagonally and gather both
layers together along both of the open sides (figure 1).
Thread the brass wire through the resulting loose fold and
hold the two ends together to form a loop. Pull the gathering
as tight as possible and secure the loop. Squeeze the tip of
the petal to form a point (figure 2). Repeat the process for
all the remaining petals.

For the stamens, thread each bead on to a piece of binding
wire and bind together. Make a bunch of five varying
lengths, twist the ends round each other and continue this
process until all the beads are in groups of five (figure 3).
Place one group of stamens into a stem so that they lie on the
gathering and join to the petal binding. Repeat this with
the remaining beads until six petals have them and nine are
left plain. Make a group of three petals with beads so that
they are back to back in the centre (figure 4). Bind these to
the stem and then add the next three with beads so that they
encase the joins of the first set of petals, with beads
uppermost and the tips pointing outwards (figure 5). The
next set of petals echoes exactly the position of the first three,
with the last six arranged in the same way as the second set.
The joins between the previous petals will provide a natural
position for this last group.

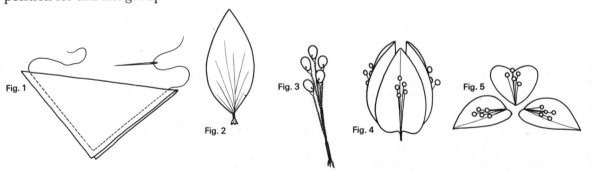

Fig. 1

Fig. 2

Fig. 3

Fig. 4

Fig. 5

# Chiffon tulip

(Pink) chiffon crêpe
Brass wire
Stem and binding wires
Tape

Cut five pieces of chiffon 18 cm (7 in) square and five pieces
of brass wire 20 cm (8 in) long. Fold one piece of chiffon in
half diagonally, twist the end of a piece of binding wire
round the brass wire and thread a needle on to the other end.
Sew all along the two open sides, stitching through both
layers of material (figure 1). Pull the gathering tight, and
thread the spare end of brass wire through the loose fold of
fabric. Push the wire until the fabric is stretched and join
the ends together to secure the loop (figure 2). Squeeze the
top into a point and fold the loop to form a trough (figure 3).
Make five of these and assemble the flower by binding each
petal with the curved brass wire on the outside to form the
flower outline.

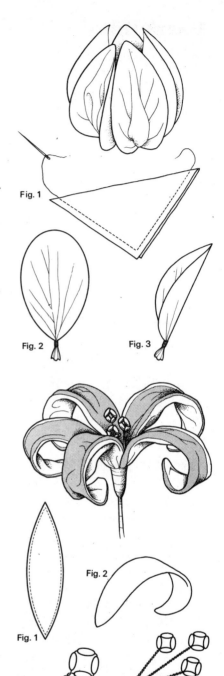

# Tiger lily

2 shades of silk
Oblong beads
Brass wire

Cut six pointed petal shapes 8·5 cm (7¼ in) long in each of
the two shades of silk. Making a pair with one of each
shade, stitch round the edge with the right side facing
inwards (figure 1). Reverse the shape to conceal the raw
edges inside. Push a loop of brass wire inside until the shape
is fully stretched and bind tightly to retain the shape.
Make up the remaining five petals similarly and gently
curve the wire of each one until the whole shape curls over
(figure 2). Thread four beads on to a piece of binding wire
and join the ends together so that the beads form a ring on a
stem (figure 3). Make three of these, bunch them together
and bind them to the stem (figure 4). Attach the petals
individually, cover the stem and bend the stem to make the
flower face forwards.

# Camellia

Chiffon crêpe
Brass wire
Stem and binding wires
Tape

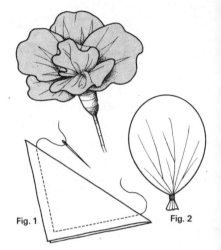

Cut six squares of crêpe 6·5 cm (2½ in) across and six pieces of brass wire 11·5 cm (4½ in) long. Fold one piece of crêpe diagonally in half and gather with binding wire along both of the free edges sewing both layers at once (figure 1). Twist the end of the wire to a piece of brass wire to anchor it before threading the brass wire between the layers of fabric. Make as large a loop as possible and secure with binding wire (figure 2). Make five more, then make three kinks in the brass wire at regular intervals. Place one petal on to the stem as the centre with five petals round it. Then twist the centre petal round until it coils gently.

Fig. 1    Fig. 2

# Patterned cone

Printed lawn    Stem and binding wires
Puff ball    Tape
Brass wire

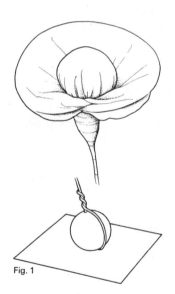

Thread the stem wire right through the puff ball if possible, twisting the end back round the stem and taking care not to distort the shape of the ball.

Cut two shapes from the printed lawn, one square, 11·5 cm (4½ in) across and the other oblong, 11·5 cm × 23 cm (4½ in × 9 in). Use the square one to cover the puff ball (figure 1), and bind tightly to gather the fabric into the stem. Use the continuing piece of binding wire and thread a needle to the end. Fold the oblong piece in half lengthways and gather the long open side, sewing both layers at once. Pull the gathering as tight as possible or until the fabric forms one circlet and finish off. Thread the brass wire all round the frill so that it stretches the fabric to the full. Pull the spare ends down into the binding before covering the stem.

Fig. 1

# Brocade leaf

Brocade
Brass wire
Stem and binding wires
Tape

Cut a pair of leaf shapes from either side of the fabric
(figure 1). Face the right sides together and stitch all round
the edge before turning it inside out. Push a piece of wire
inside to stretch the fabric. Secure the shape with wire,
cover the stem and then use the wire to shape the leaf
realistically.

Fig. 1

# Pleated leaf

Pleated chiffon
Stem and binding wires
Tape

Compress the pleats and cut strips diagonally 5 cm (2 in)
long (figure 1). Thread a piece of binding wire on to a needle
and sew straight along one edge through the folds. Shape
the wire to form a loop which allows the pleats to fan out.
Twist the ends together and bind to a stem.

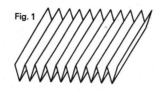

Fig. 1

# Table flower display

Table flower

Sometimes space is limited or decorations should be
restrained if an intimate occasion demands. Alternatively a
coffee table would be enhanced by a single bloom. This
brown chiffon flower is designed for such uses and in this
particular case is displayed on a blue ceramic candlestick

# Tea urn

Tiger lilies
Patterned cones
Fantasy buds
Brocade leaves

This handsome tea urn deserves the full blooms of the lilies
which really dominate the design. Intermingled with the
other components – patterned cones, fantasy buds and
brocade leaves – are some glycerined beech leaves for a
touch of reality

# Chapter eleven  Shells

There is very little shaping that is possible with shells, so the success of a shell flower design depends entirely on the choice of material. For example, from the flat cockle, abalone or capiz type of shell, leaves and flowers with flat petals can be made, while the spiral or snail types are more suited to stamens or seed centres. Cowries are a particularly beautiful, special shape and can be used for sprays, as can winkles. There are many shells which are really too large to be part of a flower and are more suitable as vases or prominent architectural features. Clams, conches and abalone in particular can be used for containers, whereas screw and sundial shells are so striking that their use as individual items are sufficient impact. Being hard in feel and outline, a softening material such as coral seafern or even some types of seaweed is an asset.

Having said that shells cannot be reshaped, it should be mentioned that they can be cut with caution. Some are more easily modified than others, but it is wise to consider the merits of a cut and, therefore, imperfect shell. For wiring facilities it is possible to drill shells and a pair of holes makes for more stable wiring than one. A tacky substance is the simplest way to assemble flowers or add stems; plasticine is excellent to use although glue may be an added asset for security.

Shells are available in little packages from all over the world if the nearest beach is not forthcoming. Craft and seaside gift shops often display a shell collection.

**Flowers**
Cockle lily
Spiral cone
Pussy willow
Capiz shell flower
Chinese lanterns
Stem of bells
Capiz rose
Capiz star

**Leaves**
Winkle wheat
Olive spray
Scallop leaf

**Display**
Shell design
Vase of shell flowers

# Cockle lily

Half a heart cockle    Glue
1 nerita             Stem wire
Plasticine         Tape

Cover the stem and make a small open hook on the top
(figure 1). Make a small ball of plasticine and place it inside
the hinge. Push the hook into this with a little glue. Then
cover up the plasticine by sticking a small nerita type of
shell over it. These are surprisingly realistic looking, and
the fact that both sides of the shell will tend to veer in their
own directions adds to the charm of irregularity.

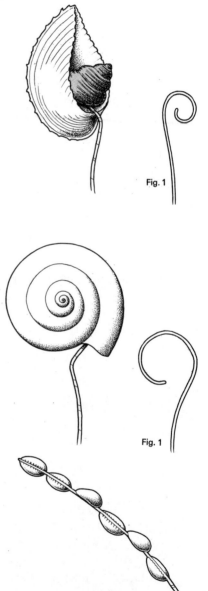

Fig. 1

# Spiral cone

Sundial shell    Stem wire
Plasticine        Tape
Glue

Cover the stem with tape and curve the top to a gentle hook
(figure 1). Take a piece of plasticine large enough to fill the
aperture. Gently push the wire into this, easing it so that it
can be felt to work its way into the spiral of the shell. The
markings on this shell are most striking and therefore could
well be displayed either way up. However, the inside of the
spiral viewed from underneath has been chosen as more
sympathetic to the conical lily shape. So bend the stem wire
accordingly as close as possible to the shell.

Fig. 1

# Pussy willow

Cowries     Glue
Stem wire   Paint
Tape

Cover the stem with tape and glue a shell on alternate sides
at intervals. Use a lacquer or shiny acrylic paint with an
oil base and paint the lower half of each shell. Cowries are
the most realistic to choose for pussy willow, but a lot of the
nerita or coiled snail type of shell would also be effective.

# Capiz shell flower

Capiz shells                    Stem wire
Verbernium or small whorl-shaped shells    Glue
Plasticine                     Tape

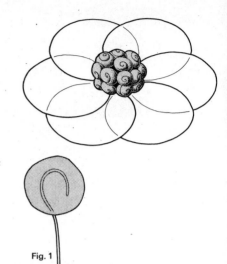

Cover the stem, bend it in half and hook it over a lump of glued plasticine (figure 1). Cover the top surface with the little shells. Push the capiz shells into the plasticine below, making sure there is enough glue to hold the shell. Arrange them so that they radiate evenly around the centre. These beautiful transparent discs from the Philippines are available in two sizes which allows for variation within an arrangement.

Fig. 1

# Chinese lanterns

5 heart cockles
Stem and binding wires
Tape

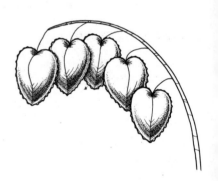

These charming shells are sold commercially, and when obtained from a shop they will most probably be tied together in pairs with ribbon or string. Their serrated edges match exactly and do not easily interlock with half of a different pair. However, undo the tie, apply glue to the serrated edge and join again, sandwiching a piece of binding wire between them. Make five of these and leave to dry. Attach the wire stems at regular intervals to the main stem binding and arch it over so that the row of hearts can hang vertically.

# Stem of bells

6 pearl beads
3 limpets
Stem and binding wires
Tape

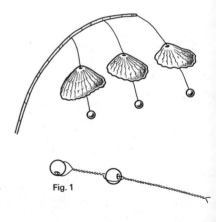

Thread each bead on to a piece of binding wire and twist the ends together for 2 cm ($\frac{3}{4}$ in), then thread a second one and repeat the process (figure 1). Use a limpet with a hole in it and thread it on to the twisted binding wire so that it rests on the bead. Make three of these and join them to the main stem, binding at regular intervals. Arch the stem over so that the pendulous little bells can hang downwards.

Fig. 1

# Capiz rose

Capiz shells  Glue
Plasticine  Tape
Stem wire

Cover the stem with tape, bend in half and hook it on to a lump of glue-coated plasticine (figure 1). Start at the top and insert the capiz shells at random. They should be facing various directions and eventually fill the whole of the plasticine. It may be necessary to apply additional glue to hold the shells in place. This is preferable to an overlarge lump of plasticine.

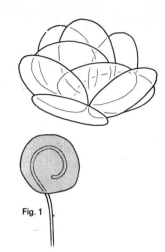

Fig. 1

# Capiz star

1 pearl
6 capiz shells
Stem and binding wires
Tape

Thread the pearl bead on to a piece of binding wire, twist the ends together to form a stem and bind it to the stem (figure 1). Using a heavy pair of scissors or florists' cutters, trim the capiz shells to a point. Firm, slow cuts will prevent the shells from shattering. Place the shells on a work surface and drill a small hole in the base of each (figure 2). Thread binding wire through the hole and twist the ends together. Wire this to the main stem. If the petals fall outwards, the neighbouring ones should keep them in place.

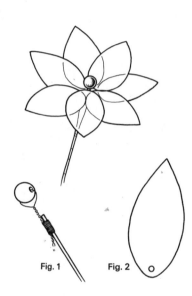

Fig. 1        Fig. 2

# Winkle wheat

6 winkles
Plasticine
Stem and binding wires

Fold six pieces of binding wire in half and fill the mouth of each winkle with plasticine. Push a wire loop into one of the plasticine-filled shells to act as a stem (figure 1). Repeat the process with the remaining five shells. Cover the stem, including a shell stem at regular intervals. Curve the whole spray gently over until there is an arch with a row of shells on the top.

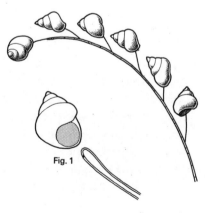

Fig. 1

# Olive spray

7 olive shells
Stem and binding wires
Tape

The spiral form of the olive shells often produces a small
notch both at the top and bottom of the lip. Shells without
this are not suitable, as the wire will not grip. Make a hook
by folding a piece of binding wire in half. Place it over the
two notches and twist the ends together very tightly to
secure the shell (figure 1). Repeat the process with the other
seven. Join the wire stems to the main one by incorporating
them at intervals to the binding. Allow the shells to have at
least 2·5 cm (1 in) of their own stem so that they stand free
of an arched main stem.

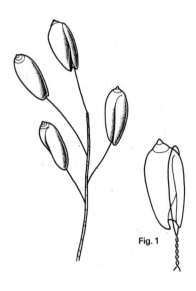

Fig. 1

# Scallop leaf

1 scallop shell
Plasticine
Stem wire

This seems a very obvious shell to choose for a leaf. It is,
but so are many others, too numerous to mention by name.
All that is needed is a flat shape, preferably to contrast with
the flowers they are to accompany. Simply roll a ball of
plasticine, and glue it to the back of the shell. Cover a stem
and make a hook in the top to push into the plasticine
(figure 1). This can be seen from one side but this is a
natural limitation.

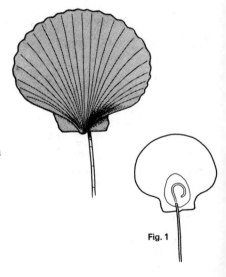

Fig. 1

# Shell design

| | |
|---|---|
| Capiz stars | Large auger shells |
| Coral | Spiral cones |
| Cockle lilies | |

Coral is a splendid foil to cover the mechanics of this design and the pile appears to support all the other material. The centre is filled with capiz stars which surround the cockle lilies and spiral cones. The vertical feeling is emphasized by three auger shells

# Vase of shell flowers

Chinese lanterns
Stem of bells
Winkle wheat
Pussy willow

The brass vase is the perfect shape for an informal display of
this kind. The stems of the Chinese lanterns and winkle
wheat arch gracefully from the vase

# Chapter twelve Wire and metal

This is not the material which first springs to mind for flowermaking, but it can be very effective. Clear, uncluttered lines of wire and metal are emphasized in the choice of flowers. Wire can be coiled and looped, but being of thin substance, a quantity of layers is often required to produce intensity of colour. With wire, stylized petal shapes are suggested by the outline created by the material. Generally there is simply space within looped petals. Striking modern designs are particularly successful with wire and metal. Copper or brass sheeting, while being extremely flexible, have their own limitations. They will score, curl and cut, or be punched, but require sympathetic direct handling to avoid kinking which happens very easily. Apart from the brass and copper sheeting which is supplied for jewellery and enamel work at craft shops, there is the choice of round and flat wire in the same two materials. Another interesting type of wire is the woolly-textured chenille wire. This is a twisted wire with fibres integrated between the wire. Available from craft shops in many colours, some is shaped in undulating lines. As an alternative, pipe cleaners would be equally effective.

Additional material, such as nuts and bolts or nails and screws, make excellent little objects for centres. In fact, a trip to a hardware shop may produce many interesting shapes to try.

**Flowers**
Punched buttercup
Copper iris
Wire flower
Wire spring flower
Chenille flower
Chenille star
Coloured wire carnation
Coloured wire violet
Coloured wire bud
Metal poinsettia
Red hot poker

**Leaves**
Coloured wire leaves
Chenille leaves
Sheet metal spiral leaves

**Display**
Jug of flowers
Brass wire flowers
Brass design
Chenille wire flowers

# Punched buttercup

Nail
Sheet copper
Stem wire
Tape

Cut a circular shape 5 cm (2 in) across with four rounded petal shapes (figure 1). Press a hole with a pointed object in the centre of each of the four petals. This will make a cup shape in each petal. Hammer a nail into the centre of the disc and pull it through until the wire holds in the centre. Bind the stem and the nail together, ensuring that there is sufficient binding below the flowerhead to support it without wobbling.

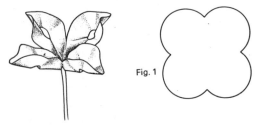

Fig. 1

# Copper iris

Copper sheeting
Stem and binding wires
Tape

Cut six pointed petal shapes 10 cm (4 in) long and make scores with a pointed instrument in parallel lines along the length of each one (figure 1). Attach the first three petals and curve them inwards to form a closed point in the centre. Then add the remaining three and curve them outwards until they curl right out and in again to touch the stem. Covering the stem may well disturb the positions of the petals, but they can always be replaced again.

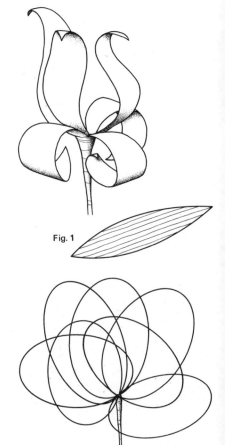

Fig. 1

# Wire flower

Brass wire
Stem and binding wires
Tape

Coil the wire to produce eight rings and hold them together with a twist of binding wire. The strength in the wire will allow the rings to spring open when they are released. Cover the stem and allow the rings to tumble at will.

# Wire spring flower

Brass wire               Piano wire
Brass nuts              Tape
Stem and binding wire

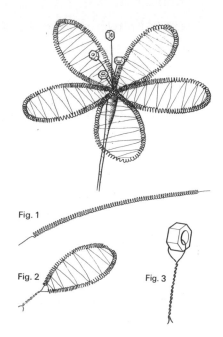

Fig. 1

Fig. 2

Fig. 3

This flower needs firm handling and a vice is useful to form a spring. It is quite possible to make one without but as several are required for one flower, holding the wire can be painful after a while. Fix the piano wire and a piece of brass wire in the vice and bind the brass wire in a tight spiral round the piano wire sixty-five times (figure 1). Release the vice and remove the piano wire. Join the two ends together to form a loop. Take the binding wire and weave a cobweb pattern using the spring as a loom (figure 2). For the stamens, thread each nut on to a separate piece of binding wire and twist the ends together to form a stem (figure 3). Attach the bunch of stamens leaving a stem of 4 cm (1½ in), then add the petals before covering the stem. Curve the petals outwards at the tips.

# Chenille flower

Chenille wire
Stem and binding wire
Tape

Make seven loops with one continuous piece of chenille wire. Thread the binding wire through the base of the petals (figure 1) and pull tightly together. Bind to the stem. Kink the end of each petal to make a heart shape and bend the last one inwards to form the centre.

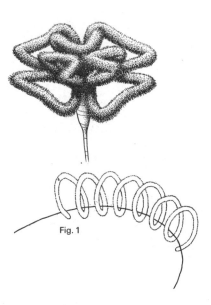

Fig. 1

# Chenille star

Shaped chenille wire
Stem and binding wires
Tape

Kink the wire at the thin points to form a zigzag of five points (figure 1). Join binding wire to the top of the stem and weave it in and out of the chenille wire. Pull it tight and the star will form itself. Ensure that the ends are well secured before binding the stem with tape.

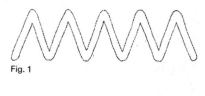

Fig. 1

# Coloured wire carnation

2 shades of coloured wire
Stem and binding wires
Tape

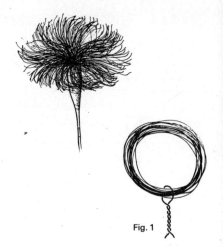

Using the index and middle fingers together, bind both colours together one hundred times around them. Remove the wire intact and secure by threading a piece of binding wire through the loops and twisting together tightly (figure 1). Join the wire twist to a stem and cover with tape. Cut the loops and ease the petals outwards to form a flat flowerhead but retain the curved ends so that the edges of the petals curve upwards.

Fig. 1

# Coloured wire violet

Coloured wire
Stem and binding wires
Tape

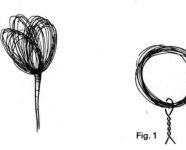

Using the index and middle fingers together, bind the coloured wire fifty times round them. Remove the wire and thread a piece of binding wire through the loops and secure by twisting the ends together (figure 1). Join to a stem and cover with tape. Ease out the loops so that they are evenly divided into four petals, and then curve two upwards and two downwards. Shape the stem so that the flower faces outwards.

Fig. 1

# Coloured wire bud

Coloured wire
Stem and binding wires
Tape

Using the index finger only, bind the coloured wire fifty times around it. Ease the wire shapes off and secure with a piece of binding wire with the ends twisted together. Join it to a stem and cover with tape. Shape the bud by twisting some of the loops round slightly until a satisfactory shape is achieved.

# Metal poinsettia

Sheet metal
Stem and binding wires
Tape

Cut six petal shapes 7·5 cm × 3 cm (3 in × 1 in) so that they are long and pointed with curved edges (figure 1). Thread three nuts on to their own individual wire stems (figure 2), and bind them to the stem. Attach the petals individually and arrange them evenly round the stamens. After the stem is covered, flatten the petals out to create a large star shape.

# Red hot poker

Chenille wire
Stem and binding wires
Tape

Make a corkscrew which starts very tight, gets fatter in the centre and tightens to a point at the tip (figure 1). Leave a spare piece to attach to the stem, first with wire and then tape.

# Coloured wire leaves

Coloured wire
Stem wire
Tape

Using the index and middle fingers together, bind the wire round them ten times. Release the rings and twist them into a figure '8' to form the base and tip of a leaf (figure 1). Make five leaves and join them to a stem, one at the top with the others alternating down the stem.

# Chenille leaves

Chenille wire
Stem and binding wire
Tape

Cut five pieces of chenille wire, one 5 cm (2 in) and the others 17 cm (7 in) long. Make a loop with the short piece (figure 1) and bind it with wire to the top of the stem. Cover the binding and a short length of stem with tape. Join one of the long pieces into a ring, then twist the centre to form a figure '8' (figure 2). Bind this to the stem and cover with tape. Add the remaining leaves similarly before closing the loops together and arching the stem gently.

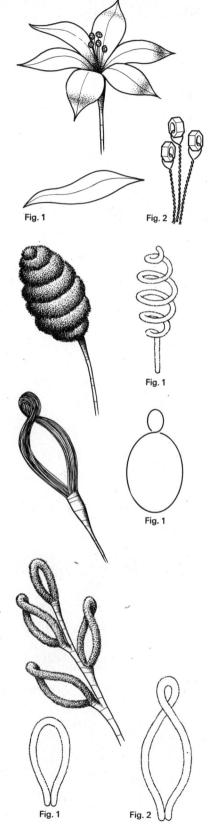

Fig. 1

Fig. 2

Fig. 1

Fig. 1

Fig. 1

Fig. 2

# Sheet metal spiral leaves

Brass sheeting
Stem wire
Tape

Cut a long, thin, pointed shape and score several lines with
a pointed instrument along the length. Make the lines
converge at the point of the leaf; the number will depend
on the proportion of the leaf (figure 1). Join the base of the
leaf, coil it round the stem, and cover with tape. The long
pointed shape is an invitation for a variety of shapes, from
a corkscrew to a large, undulating curl.

# Jug of flowers (below left)

Punched buttercups
Iris
Poinsettia

This jug is filled with metal flowers of sheet copper and
brass. The scored texture adds an interesting quality to
relieve the stiff appearance of untreated metal

Fig. 1

# Brass wire flowers (above right)

Wire spring flowers
Brass tendrils

The two wire flowers are the most important components
in this design. Brass tendrils tumble and curl between the
flowers

114

# Brass design (below left)

Wire flowers
Tendrils

A classical brass cylinder is an invitation for a striking yet
simple design. The materials used are brass, like the
container, with the tendrils extending the line of flowers

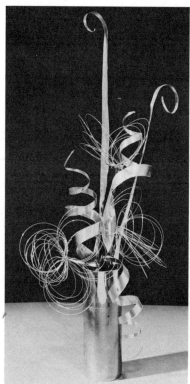 

# Chenille wire flowers (above right)

Chenille wire flowers
Red hot pokers
Chenille stars
Chenille leaves

The profile of the red hot pokers are easily definable
between the sprays of leaves and stars. The centre is
emphasized by the three flowers which nestle on the top of
the glass vase

# Chapter thirteen Wood

It is natural to assume that wood is inflexible and is a heavy
clumsy material to work with. Yes, it is, but there are strips
of wood shavings available which can be soaked and
reshaped in their wet flexible state. When dry, the new
form will retain its shape with surprising resilience. The
point at which the term 'wood' ceases to be the stem and
trunk of a tree and is simply the hard texture of, say, a cane
or fircone, is debatable. Since the latter have found a place
with the dried plant material, the flowers and designs
which follow are made with wood shavings, chips and sticks.

**Flowers**
Daisy
Rose
Hypericum

**Leaves**
Stick leaf
Grass
Wooden quilled leaves

**Display**
Daisies in grass
Trailing stem

## Daisy

2 shades of mosaic chips
Card disc    Tape
Stem wire    Glue

Cut a small disc of paper 2·5 cm (1 in) in diameter and coat
one surface with glue. Cover the stem with tape, make a
hook on the top and place it on the disc (figure 1). Attach
one shade of mosaic chips as the petals. A little more glue is
then required to attach the contrasting piece in the centre.

Fig. 1

# Rose

2 shades of wood mosaic chips
Styrofoam ball    Tape
Stem wire         Glue

Cover the stem wire and glue the styrofoam ball on the top.
Push the corners of the mosaic chips into the styrofoam with
a little glue to secure each one (figure 1). Make two
circlets of petals leaving the centre free. Use the second
shade of chips and lie these flat, with glue, at the centre of
the flower.

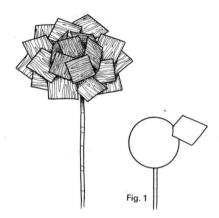

Fig. 1

# Hypericum

Wooden beads      Tape
Wood shavings     Glue
Stem and binding wires

Thread each bead on to a piece of binding wire and twist
the ends together to secure the position (figure 1). Dampen
the whole roll of wood shavings and leave rolled over a
cotton reel to dry. Cut the strip into lengths of 8·5 cm
(3½ in) and trim the ends to rounded points. Coil a short
strip to form a cone, thread the stem through the centre and
secure with glue (figure 2). Attach each of the petals to the
outside of the cone with glue. The weight of the flowerhead
will almost certainly require extra stems for support.

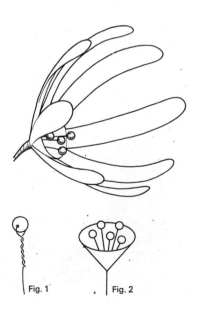

Fig. 1        Fig. 2

117

## Stick leaf

Wooden sticks
Stem and binding wires
Tape

Fold a piece of binding wire in half, place a wooden stick in the fold, and twist the wire together to hold the wood in position (figure 1). Repeat this several times until a line of parallel sticks are trapped between twisted wires. Bind the twisted ends to a stem wire. Trim the sticks to a leaf shape and curve the wire to make the leaf undulate.

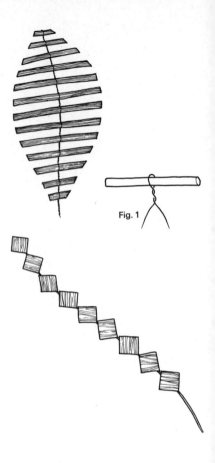

Fig. 1

## Grass

Mosaic chips
Stem wire
Tape
Glue

First cover the stem wire with tape and then put a thin line of glue along one side of the stem leaving 5 cm (2½ in) spare at the bottom. Place the chips on to the glue and leave on a flat surface to dry so that they are all on a similar plane.

## Wooden quilled leaves

Wood shaving strips
Stem wires
Tape
Glue

Dampen the wood shaving strip, roll it up tightly, secure with sticky tape and leave to dry (figure 1). Make at least five and remove tape before sticking to a covered stem wire. Allow the spirals to unroll and spring freely.

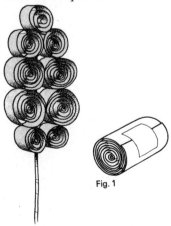

Fig. 1

# Daisies in grass

Daisies
Grass
Wooden sticks

Sometimes the simplicity of material suggests a similar
feeling in design. The daisies here find their way between
the long grass whilst the wooden sticks suggest a carpet of
short grass

# Trailing stem

Roses
Stick leaves

Making flowers on wire stems provides a flexibility beyond
the possibility of real plant material. This stoneware
container on the wall provides anchorage for this simple
display of little wooden flowers

# Chapter fourteen  Miscellaneous

**Flowers**
Leather rose
Organdie rose
Organdie lily
Organdie stephanotis
Hessian ribbon flower
Felt forget-me-nots
Tissue paper rose
Tissue paper aster

**Leaves**
Leather leaf
Tissue paper fern
Hessian leaf

**Display**
Organdie wedding bouquet
Leather corsage
Hessian wreath
Felt victorian posy

Here is a miscellany of materials, each of which earn
themselves inclusion in this book, but do not necessarily
merit a whole chapter of their own. Fabrics such as felt,
hessian and organdie have individual qualities to enhance
a floral design. Tissue papers and leather act as a contrast
and are also individually useful. Each material will have its
own limitations and possibilities which are incorporated
into the design.

## Leather rose

Pieces of suede
Cotton wool
Stem and binding wires
Tape

Take a piece of cotton wool and roll it into a ball. Make a
hook on the top of a stem wire and insert the cotton wool
before tightening the wires together to twist them and
secure them (figure 1). Place a piece of leather over the
cotton wool and fold the sides over each other to form a
cone shape before binding the edges into the stem. Cut nine
rounded petal shapes 5 cm × 7·5 cm (2 in × 3 in).
Attach each petal individually, stretching the leather so
that each petal encases the previous ones. When the stem is
covered, ease the tops of the petals so that they curl
outwards.

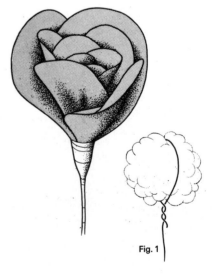

Fig. 1

# Organandie rose

Organdie
Stem and binding wires
Tape

Cut eleven pairs of rounded petal shapes 5 cm × 4 cm
(2 in × 1½ in) (figure 1), and curl the tops of the petals
outwards. Cut one square piece 7·5 cm (3 in) across and
fold it in half diagonally. Coil the side corners over the
centre one to form a cone (figure 2). Bind it to the stem and
attach the petals separately making a pleat in the base of
each one to form a cup in the centre. Each petal should
overlap the previous one as the layers build up.

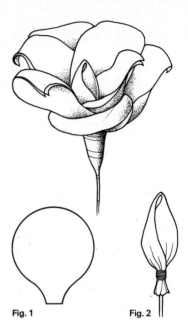

Fig. 1    Fig. 2

# Organandie lily

Pearls
Organdie
Stem and binding wires
Tape

These petals are made with a triple layer of fabric, so cut
three pointed petal shapes 9·5 cm × 5·5 cm (3¾ in × 2¼ in)
(figure 1). Thread one bead on to a piece of binding wire
and twist the end back on to the other. Then thread on the
remaining beads (figure 2) and secure them, covering the
stem. Use the double petal layers as one, and coil the
sides round and the tip over. Bind them to the stem, coiling
them round so that they overlap the stamen in the front.

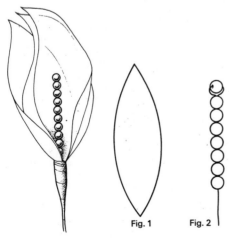

Fig. 1    Fig. 2

# Organdie stephanotis

Pearl bead
Organdie
Stem and binding wires
Tape

Cut a single shape with four petals 3·5 cm (1¼ in) across
(figure 1). Thread the bead on to a piece of binding wire
and twist the ends together to secure the position (figure 2).
Thread the stem through the centre and cover the stem with
tape to secure the position. With the fingernail, curl the
edges of the petals upwards so that the small flower is
cup-shaped.

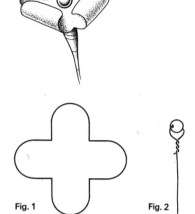

Fig. 1          Fig. 2

# Hessian ribbon flower

Hessian ribbon 7·5 cm (3 in) wide
Stem and binding wires
Tape

Cut one piece of ribbon 10 cm (4 in) and six others 9·5 cm
(3¾ in) long. Roll the first piece into a tight spiral and bind
it to the top of a stem wire (figure 1). Cut the other pieces
to pointed petal shapes. Cover six stem wires, apply glue to
the entire top surface of the petals, lie the wires from point
to point and leave to dry (figure 2). Bind the wire stems to
the stem and curl the petals outwards. Apply additional
glue to the tip and squeeze together, holding the shape with
a paper clip until it is dry.

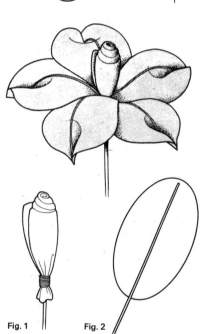

Fig. 1          Fig. 2

# Felt forget-me-nots

Stamens
Felt
Stem and binding wires
Tape

Cut a shape of four petals with rounded edges (figure 1).
The stamens normally are made double, with a seed on
either end. As only one is needed, simply cut through the
thread in the centre. Bind the single seed to a stem. Make a
small hole in the centre of one of the petal discs and thread
it on to the stem and cover the stem to secure the position
of the petals. Repeat the process for the other three flowers
and make a bunch of them. Keeping the flowerheads level,
bind them together and cover as one stem.

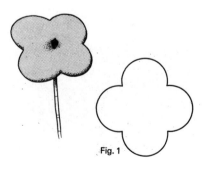

Fig. 1

# Tissue paper rose

3 shades of tissue paper
Stem and binding wires
Tape

Fold each shade of tissue into layers and, taking the palest
first, cut all the layers at once to a rounded petal shape
5 cm × 6·5 cm (2 in × 2½ in) (figure 1). Then, using that as
a pattern, cut the next shade 1 cm (½ in) larger all round.
Repeat the process for the third and largest set of petals.
Join the binding wire to the stem and taking one of the
small pale petals, roll it up into a tight tube and attach it to
the stem (figure 2). Add five more individual petals coiling
each one round the previous ones. From then on, all the
remaining petals are added in pairs, and each should have a
slight pleat in the base to prevent it tearing and
consequently falling open. When all the petals are
assembled, cover the stem, then curl as many of the petals
outwards as possible, starting with the outside ones.

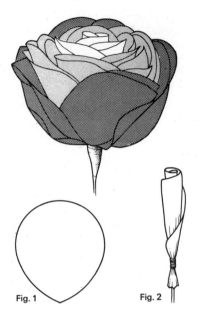

Fig. 1            Fig. 2

# Tissue paper aster

3 shades of tissue paper
Stem and binding wires
Tape

Fold the tissue paper until there are twelve layers. Do this
with each colour and cut a square 21·5 cm (8½ in) across.
Attach the binding wire to the stem and make a hook on
the top (figure 1). Coil all the layers of tissue, as though
they were one, around the stem. Hold them in place with
the binding wire during the process of binding. The result is
a fat cigarette shape (figure 2). Cover the stem and then
make cuts down the roll to within 2·5 cm (1 in) of the
binding to make strips of petals. Separate the layers and
allow them to tumble at will. Curl the ends of the petals in
various directions.

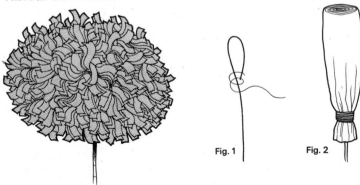

Fig. 1            Fig. 2

# Leather leaf

Suede
Stem wire
Glue
Tape

Cut a simple leaf shape (figure 1). Cover the stem wire and apply glue along one side equal to the length of the leaf. Lie it on the shiny side and leave it to dry. Use the wire support to curve and create an undulating leaf shape.

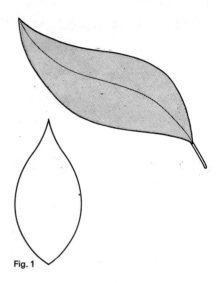

Fig. 1

# Tissue paper fern

2 shades of tissue paper
Stem wire
Glue

Cut fourteen layers of each shade into long pointed leaf shapes with flat bases 38 cm × 7·5 cm (15 in × 3 in) (figure 1). Cover the stem wire, draw a line of glue up the centre of the leaf and place the wire on it. Then build up the layers using alternate colours and applying a line of glue on top of the previous one each time. Make rows of cuts into the stem on either side to make a fish bone pattern (figure 2). Curl all the separate layers and shape the wire to a double curve with the top curling right over.

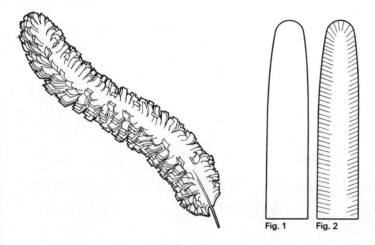

Fig. 1    Fig. 2

# Hessian leaf

Hessian
Stem wire
Tape

Cut a serrated thistle-shaped leaf (figure 1). Cover the stem wire and apply glue to one side, equal to the length of the leaf. Place the wire on the back and leave to dry before using the wire to curve the leaf into an undulating shape. Draw a tiny line of glue all round the edge to prevent fraying.

Fig. 1

# Organdie wedding bouquet (below)

Organdie roses
Organdie lilies
Organdie stephanotis

The most delicate of fabrics, organdie has that special quality of strength with translucency. It is therefore one of the traditional materials for wedding work. Both as headdresses or sprays to carry, the addition of pearls and silk ribbon is really all that is required to achieve the correct balance of materials

## Leather corsage (right)

Leather roses
Leather leaves

This subtle corsage will enhance winter
jackets, hats or handbags. Just a few
small off-cuts can be used to good
advantage for this spray

## Hessian wreath (below)

Hessian ribbon flowers
Hessian leaves
Ribbon

A brightly coloured wreath on the front
door or in a hallway is a warm,
cheerful welcome for visitors. The bright,
clear colours of orange and green
dominate this display

# Felt victorian posy

Felt forget-me-nots

This charming way of arranging a cluster of flowers was a favourite of the Victorians. Traditionally the posy is a tightly packed dome of flowers arranged in circles of tiny flowers which gradually deepend in tone. There are many variations on this theme but it is nice to imitate the original with little felt forget-me-nots

# Chapter fifteen  Mixtures

There are times when a combination of more than one material can provide just the right effect to give a perfect design. Using one type of material alone can be simple both to shop for and to make, but it is often an additional material which can relieve the monotony. Dried grasses and seeds make centres for various petals, providing interesting and intricate detail to the flowers just as they do when used as leaves in a complete flower arrangement. Beads are another source for stamens for fabric flowers, while ready-made stamens are also suitable.

It is advisable to be like a squirrel and always keep a collection of odds and ends; a source to draw from may just provide the suitable contrast required.

**Flowers**
Harebell
Calico poppy
Cone and hessian flower
Passion flower
Wired foil star

**Display**
Cork panel
Dried plants and feathers

## Harebell

1 harestail grass
10 gypsy sequins
Glue

This little flower is made like the dried flowers but with the gypsy sequins replacing the dried petals. Apply glue to a gypsy sequin and push it between the layers of the grass (figure 1). Make two circlets of petals in this way. The weight of the completed flowerhead will arch the stem gracefully. A wire stem could, of course, be added if required for adaptability.

Fig. 1

# Calico poppy

Teasel       Hook of wire
Calico ribbon    Tape
Stem and binding wires

Attach the teasel to a stem. Cut six rounded petal shapes 6·5 cm × 8 cm (2½ in × 3¼ in). Heat the wire hook and press into the petal shapes all along the tops to create a frilled appearance. Make a pleat in the base of one and wire it to the stem around the teasel. Then add the remaining petals similarly until all are assembled and arrange them so that they radiate evenly.

# Cone and hessian flower

Hessian     Tape
Cone        Glue
7 stem and binding wires

Cut twelve pointed petal shapes 13 cm × 5 cm (5 in × 2 in) with pinking scissors (figure 1). Cover six stem wires with tape and apply glue to the entire under-suface of six of the petals. Place the wires on the centre of each and cover with unglued petals. Use the last stem wire to put a stem on the fircone; the wired petals can then be twisted to it. When the flower is assembled, shape the petals so that they bulge out and curl in again over the fircone.

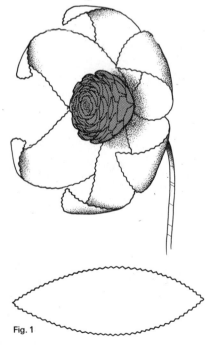

Fig. 1

# Passion flower

2 shades of metallic ribbon
Stem and binding wires
Tape

Cut six strips of one shade 6·5 cm (2½ in) long and cut into them until they are comb-shaped (figure 1). Coil one of the strips into a tight roll and bind to a stem (figure 2). Repeat the process with the other strips and bind all the stems together in a tight cluster to form the centre (figure 3). Cut six strips from the other shade with pointed ends 8 cm (3¼ in) long. Make a pleat in the bottom of one pointed petal and wire it to the stem. Add the remaining petals in a similar way, securing with a little glue if they don't stay in position.

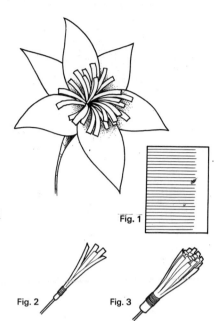

Fig. 1

Fig. 2          Fig. 3

# Wired foil star

Metallic ribbon
Wired foil
Stem and binding wires
Tape

Cut six pieces of wired foil 15 cm (6 in) long and fold them in half. Bind them to the stem with wire. Separate the stamens and curve them all outwards at the tip (figure 1). Cut six pointed petals 7 cm × 4 cm (2¾ in × 1½ in), then apply glue to six pieces of covered stem wire and attach one to the back of each petal. Join these to the stem and use the wire to create an undulating curve.

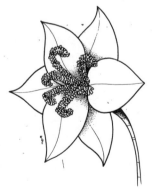

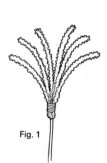

Fig. 1

# Cork panel

Cone and hessian flowers
Dried mahonia leaves
Fircones
Corn

The texture of cork is an excellent background for the
cluster of flowers with dried grasses displayed on this panel.
A design of this kind can hang vertically or horizontally
according to the available space

# Dried plants and feathers

Feather lily cocquilles
Feather pointed bird of paradise flowers

Dried plants contrast yet enhance the gentle flimsy quality
of feathers, yet the fact that they are both natural materials
gives them a special lasting quality. This particular design
is made in shades of green with the few black harestail
grasses emphasizing the colour of the wrought iron

# Chapter sixteen
# Useful addresses

| | |
|---|---|
| Papers | Paperchase,<br>216 Tottenham Court Road,<br>London W1 |
| Beads | Ells & Farrier,<br>2 Princess Street,<br>Hanover Square,<br>London W1 |
| Feathers<br>Flowermaking materials:<br>tape, wires (stem,<br>binding and chenille),<br>flower irons,<br>flowermaking kits | Inflower,<br>The Studio,<br>Holwell,<br>Sherborne,<br>Dorset |
| Pamela Woods craft kits | Inflower,<br>The Studio,<br>Holwell,<br>Sherborne,<br>Dorset |
| Pots | Bob Parkes,<br>Ceramics,<br>30 St Mary's Row,<br>Moseley,<br>Birmingham B13 8JG |
| Ribbons | Lion Ribbon Co,<br>Lower Fielde,<br>Ichnor, Chichester,<br>Sussex<br><br>Lion Ribbon Co,<br>225 Fifth Avenue,<br>New York 10010 |
| Brass containers | Stuart Houghton Ltd,<br>Newton Place,<br>Factory Road,<br>Hockley, Birmingham |

| | |
|---|---|
| Hessian (burlap), felt etc., leather thonging | Tweedy Products, 26/45 Cheltenham Street, Bath, Avon |
| Raffia, stamens | Fred Aldous Ltd, PO 135, 37 Lever Street, Manchester M60 1UX |
| Dried flowers and plant material, flower wires, florist tapes | Florists |
| Wrought iron | Mike Malleson, Hempsyke, Bishop's Caundle, Sherborne, Dorset |